MAKE it WORK!

ANCIENT
EGYPT

Andrew Haslam

Consultant: George Hart, B.A. M.Phil.
The British Museum, London

MINNETONKA, MINNESOTA

Published by Two-Can Publishing
11571 K-Tel Drive
Minnetonka, MN 55343
www.two-canpublishing.com

© 2001, 1995 Two-Can Publishing

Editor: Kate Graham
Assistant editor: Jacqueline McCann
Series concept and original design: Andrew Haslam
Design: Helen McDonagh
Assistant model-maker: Sarah Davies

hc ISBN 1-58728-307-7
sc ISBN 1-58728-300-X

Photographic credits:
British Museum: 4 (tr), 12, 15, 23 (tr), 24, 28, 31, 36, 40, 41, 50 (bl), 51, 55, 58 (r);
Greg Evans International: 56, 58 (tl); Griffiths Institute: 11, 14, 37 (tr), 46, 60, 61; G.S.F. Picture Library: 39 (mr);
Image Bank: 5 (tr); Mel Pickering: 4 (map); Metropolitan Museum of Art: 52 (l); Still Pictures: 9;
Robert Harding: 23 (br) 37 (tl), 44, 50 (tl), 54, 58 (bl), RH/British Museum: 48; Science Photo Library: 39 (bl);
Wernar Forman Archive: 35; WFA/University College London, Petrie Museum: 10; WFA/British Museum: 5 (bl), 18, 47,
WFA/E Strouhal: 38; WFA/Egyptian Museum, Turin: 42; WFA/Egyptian Museum, Cairo: 52 (r).

All other photographs by Jon Barnes

Printed in China by WKT

Contents

Words marked in **bold** in the text can be found in the glossary.

Studying Egyptian Life

All human beings need food and shelter to survive. They also need things to look forward to that give their lives hope and meaning. Throughout history, different groups of people around the world have come up with their own ways of meeting these basic needs. Studying past **civilizations** can tell us how people used the resources around them to build shelters, how they farmed or found food, and how they met their spiritual needs and hopes for a better future.

△ *Simple farming methods involving oxen trampling grain were used by the Egyptians.*

▽ *This map shows modern-day Egypt and its neighbors, some of which were of major importance to ancient Egypt.*

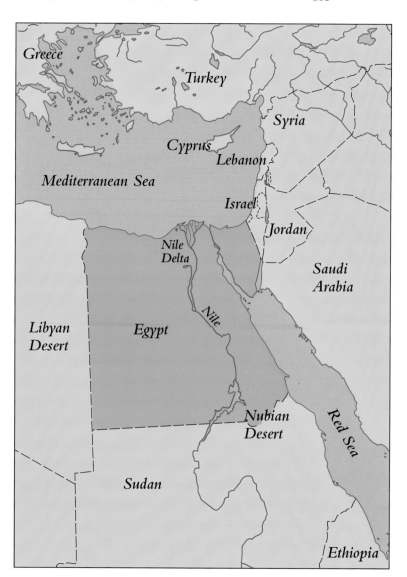

IN THE COURSE OF HISTORY civilizations have risen and eventually fallen because of internal troubles or pressures from outside. The story of the ancient Egyptian civilization is a very long one. It lasted for over 2,000 years. The Roman Empire rose and fell in half that time, and the ancient Greek civilization lasted less than 1,000 years.

TO HELP people make sense of this vast stretch of time, the greatest period of Egyptian history is usually divided into three periods, or kingdoms. In this book we have given each kingdom a symbol, which is used purely as a guide, when information relates to that time.

KEY FOR SYMBOLS

Old Kingdom 2686 B.C. – 2181 B.C.

Middle Kingdom 2055 B.C. – 1650 B.C.

⌇⌇⌇ New Kingdom 1550 B.C. – 1069 B.C.

EGYPT'S GEOGRAPHICAL LOCATION plays a vital part in understanding its development as a civilization. During the period covered in this book, foreign trade and travel grew with the discovery of valuable raw materials from abroad.

THE EGYPTIANS traveled to nearby countries by sea or over land. As the wealthiest country of the ancient world, Egypt had much to offer its neighbors, such as gold from the Eastern Desert, in exchange for what it lacked. This made for good trading relations at first, but later led to invasion by foreign countries eager to exploit Egypt's fine natural resources.

EGYPT'S LEGACY to the world lies in the most spectacular monuments ever built. The **pyramids** at Giza, the Great Sphinx, and magnificent temples are all wonderful technological achievements. In fact, experts are still trying to understand how the Egyptians were able to build such massive constructions with very simple tools.

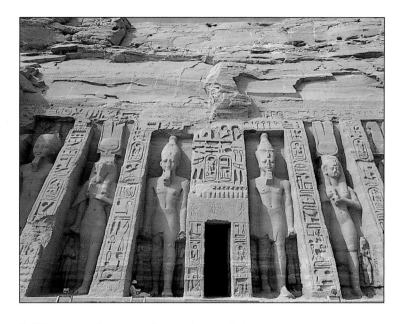

△ The magnificent temple at Abu Simbel was carved out of sandstone cliffs in the Nubian Desert on the orders of Ramses II.

ARCHAEOLOGISTS AND ANTHROPOLOGISTS have, however, been able to explain a lot about the daily life of the ancient Egyptians by the wall paintings, documents, treasures, personal possessions, and household items that have been discovered in the remains of tombs and temples.

THESE FINDINGS also reveal much about the Egyptians' religious faith and their views on death and what followed. Experts have been able to work out a lot about their belief in the **afterlife** from the discovery of tomb models buried with the dead, coffins covered with written spells to protect against danger, and **mummies**— perfectly preserved bodies for burial.

◁ This wall painting shows the type of boats the ancient Egyptians used, the birds found on the banks of the Nile, and the tools that noblemen used for hunting.

THE MAKE IT WORK! way of looking at history is to ask questions about the past and to find the answers by making the things people made as close as possible to the way they made them. You do not have to make everything in the book to understand the ancient Egyptians' way of life—in fact, just by looking at the step-by-step instructions, you will be able to see how they put things together and made them work efficiently.

Timeline

In this book we look at history by finding out how ancient Egyptians lived. Another way to look at history is to study the events and political changes that occurred over time. You can see from this chart, for instance, which dynasty of **pharaohs**, or kings, was on the throne, when Egypt started trading with other countries and when foreign invaders arrived.

EGYPTIANS WERE RULED by pharaohs and the throne was passed down through the family from generation to generation. A dynasty, or family line, continued until the male line died out and an outsider, possibly with the support of the army or court, married the queen or heiress. There was rarely a struggle. Each dynasty had its own traditions and character. Some built monuments, some encouraged the arts, some were weak and lazy, and others financed powerful armies which carried out impressive military campaigns.

B.C.

3000 · 2900 · 2800 · 2700 · 2600 · 2500 · 2400 · 2300 · 2200 · 2100 · 2000 · 1900 · 1800 · 1700

PHARAOHS

▲ The Red Crown and the White Crown symbolize the unification of Upper and Lower Egypt into one country ▼

▲ First Dynasty begins with the first pharaoh, Menes ▼

▲ Internal unrest. Old Kingdom collapses. Many less powerful pharaohs rule small territories ▼

▲ Great pharaohs of Middle Kingdom, such as Amenemhat, rule ▼

BUILDING AND TECHNOLOGY

▲ Art and hieroglyphic writing develops in Egypt ▼ Simple clothing worn

▲ First pyramids built ▼ Decorated tombs for nobles

▲ Smaller pyramid building (1800 B.C.) ▼

▲ First obelisk built (1950 B.C.) ▼

▲ Fortresses built to secure Egypt's defenses ▼

TRADE AND WAR

▲ Contact with Mediterranean Sea peoples—from Cyprus, Rhodes, and Crete—and to the East ▼

▲ Expeditions south to Nubia and Sudan ▼

▲ Trading for jewels and cedar trees begins with Lebanon, Byblos, and Somalia ▼

▲ Conquest of Nubia. Many Nubians enslaved by the Egyptians ▼

OLD KINGDOM (2686 B.C.–2181 B.C.)

INTERMEDIATE PERIOD

MIDDLE KINGDOM (2055 B.C.–1650 B.C.)

EACH KINGDOM—Old, Middle, and New— witnessed a succession of ruling dynasties. Between the kingdoms themselves there were periods of chaos and conflict. This was because of political unrest within Egypt, with a number of different rulers fighting for control of the country, and foreign invasion. After the New Kingdom ended, there were only brief periods of calm and prosperity as repeated raids from Sudan, Persia, and Macedonia became increasingly threatening and disruptive.

EGYPT FINALLY FELL to the Greeks in 332 B.C. For the next 300 years the Ptolemy family ruled the country, and important people adopted Greek **culture** and learned to speak Greek. By 30 B.C., Egypt had become a province of Rome. Over the next several hundred years the gradual erosion of Egyptian culture and religion continued. An Arab invasion of A.D. 7 saw the arrival of Islam and in A.D. 324, Egypt officially turned to Christianity replacing all the country's temples with **Coptic** churches and monasteries.

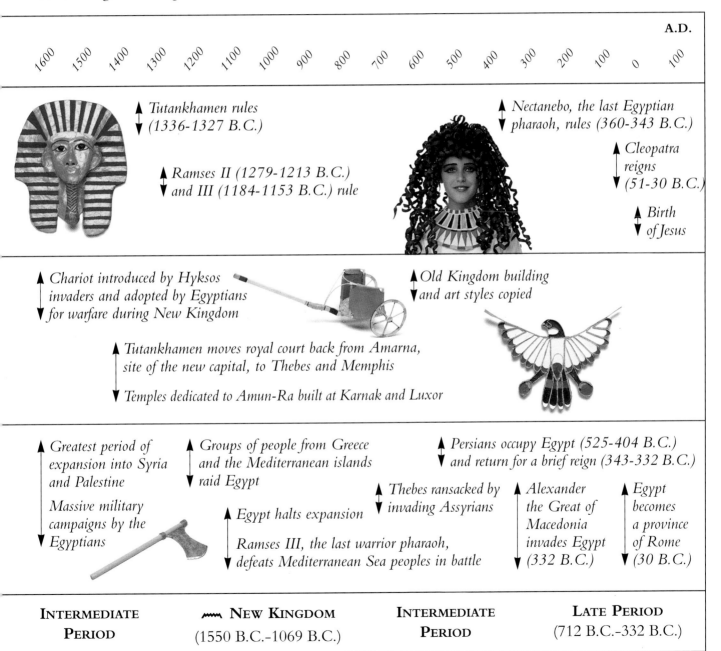

A.D.

1600 1500 1400 1300 1200 1100 1000 900 800 700 600 500 400 300 200 100 0 100

Tutankhamen rules (1336-1327 B.C.)

Nectanebo, the last Egyptian pharaoh, rules (360-343 B.C.)

Ramses II (1279-1213 B.C.) and III (1184-1153 B.C.) rule

Cleopatra reigns (51-30 B.C.)

Birth of Jesus

Chariot introduced by Hyksos invaders and adopted by Egyptians for warfare during New Kingdom

Old Kingdom building and art styles copied

Tutankhamen moves royal court back from Amarna, site of the new capital, to Thebes and Memphis

Temples dedicated to Amun-Ra built at Karnak and Luxor

Greatest period of expansion into Syria and Palestine

Groups of people from Greece and the Mediterranean islands raid Egypt

Persians occupy Egypt (525-404 B.C.) and return for a brief reign (343-332 B.C.)

Massive military campaigns by the Egyptians

Thebes ransacked by invading Assyrians

Alexander the Great of Macedonia invades Egypt (332 B.C.)

Egypt becomes a province of Rome (30 B.C.)

Egypt halts expansion

Ramses III, the last warrior pharaoh, defeats Mediterranean Sea peoples in battle

| INTERMEDIATE PERIOD | 〜〜〜 NEW KINGDOM (1550 B.C.-1069 B.C.) | INTERMEDIATE PERIOD | LATE PERIOD (712 B.C.-332 B.C.) |

The Fertile Nile River

The first Egyptians were **Stone Age** hunters, followed by settlers from the south and east who were attracted by the river valley's fertile soil. The ancient Egyptian civilization began over 5,000 years ago and lasted for more than 2,000 years before being wiped out by foreign invasions. Initially Egypt was divided into Upper and Lower Egypt (the valley and the **delta**). These were united in 3118 B.C. and ruled by a pharaoh called "Lord of the Two Lands."

▽ *The compass shows the direction of the flow of the Nile: south to north.*

▽ *Lower Egypt (Ta-mehu)*

Giza

Memphis

Nile Delta

THE MARSHY, TRIANGULAR DELTA of Lower Egypt, where the river divides into separate branches, was known as *Ta-mehu*—land of the papyrus plant. Upper Egypt, the long, narrow valley just 7 miles wide, was called *Ta-shema*—land of the reed. Ancient Egyptian civilization developed in these two fertile areas.

MEMPHIS was one of the most inhabited areas, not only of Egypt, but of the ancient world. It was the capital of Egypt during the Old Kingdom and its harbor and workshops played a key part in the country's foreign trade. Just south of Memphis is Giza, the site of the largest pyramid of all—the Great Pyramid.

THE NILE starts high in the mountains of Central Africa and springs of Ethiopia. From there it flows north to the Mediterranean Sea. Summer rains caused the Nile to flood, covering the valley floor with a layer of mud and water. When the floodwaters went down, a rich layer of soil was left behind. This soil made excellent farming land.

▷ *Today, the floodwaters of the Nile are controlled by a dam at Aswan, but a lush green corridor of rich farm land still runs along both sides of the river's banks..*

Nile   Kemet

▽ *Upper Egypt (Ta-shema)*

Aswan

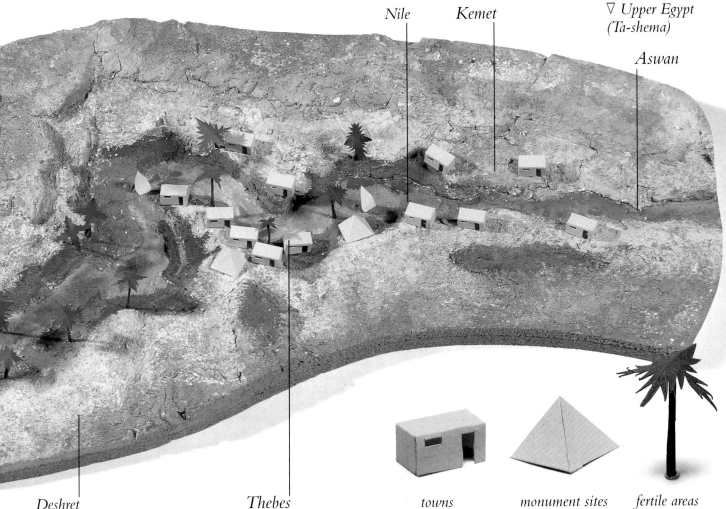

Deshret   *Thebes*   *towns*   *monument sites*   *fertile areas*

THE RED LAND or *Deshret* was the desert that surrounded the river valley. There was nothing to sustain life and nobody lived there. For the ancient Egyptians, however, it provided several things: a barrier against invasion, safe trade routes to the rest of Africa, sandstone for building monuments, and gold for making jewelry.

THE BLACK LAND, known as *Kemet*, was the narrow strip of **silt** that runs along the river valley. It took its name from the rich, fertile soil in which crops flourished. The Egyptians called themselves *remet-en-Kemet*—people of the black land—and their language, *medet-remet-en-Kemet*, meant speech of the people of the black land.

Clothing

The clothes worn by the ancient Egyptians were light and cool. They were made from fine, undyed linen cloth and needed very little stitching as they were simply draped around the body. Color and decoration came in the form of elaborate jewelry, wigs, and makeup. No one wore underwear, and because it was so hot for most of the year, children often wore nothing at all.

OLD KINGDOM WOMEN wore a simple tube dress made from a rectangle of linen sewn down one side, with straps attached to the top edge. This simple dress style did not change, although during the Middle Kingdom colorful, patterned collars started being worn by both the rich and poor. New Kingdom fashion was more elegant, with a pleated, fringed robe worn over the tube dress.

MEN WORE SHORT KILTS to the knee during the Old Kingdom. The linen cloth was pleated and fastened at the waist, either with a knot or buckle. In the Middle Kingdom, the style of kilts changed to become straight and longer for all. Full-length cloaks kept winter chills at bay.

△ *This pleated dress is possibly the oldest existing garment in the world. It dates from the period of the first pharaoh, which was around 3000 B.C.*

By the New Kingdom, fringing and pleating became popular, adorning the sashes and aprons that men now wore.

MAKE A TUNIC

You will need: needle and thread, felt-tip pen, scissors, safety pin, fabric (5 x 3 ft.)

1 Wrap the fabric around the person you are making the tunic for, from under the arms to the knees.

2 Allow an overlap of at least half the width again. Mark the fabric and cut it. Use the leftover material to make two straps.

3 Use a safety pin to hold the tube together, by pinning it carefully at the top of the back (so that you can take it off and put it on).

MAKE A PAIR OF SANDALS

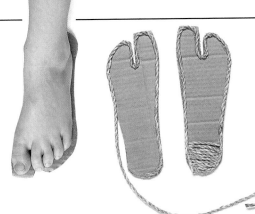

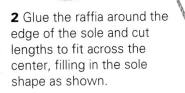

You will need: cardboard (1 x 1 ft.), pen, scissors, thin string, darning needle, glue, braided raffia

1 Place feet on the cardboard; draw around them carefully and cut out.

2 Glue the raffia around the edge of the sole and cut lengths to fit across the center, filling in the sole shape as shown.

3 Use thin string and needle to sew raffia straps into place. Fix the center of the strap between the toes and either side of the heel. Leave the rest to tie around the ankle.

PLEATING was the main form of decoration. The pleats were probably made by pressing the fabric onto a grooved board. Then they were attached with a form of starch.

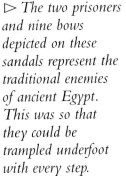

▷ *This is the kind of tunic dress that would have been worn by a servant in a noble household.*

4 Sew the straps onto both shoulders and even up the hem using a pair of scissors.

5 By adding some elaborate decoration to the basic tunic you can transform it into a costume fit for royalty. Popular decorations of the time included feathers, rosettes, and sequins. A fringed border was also used to embellish the robes of noblewomen.

▷ *The two prisoners and nine bows depicted on these sandals represent the traditional enemies of ancient Egypt. This was so that they could be trampled underfoot with every step.*

LINEN WAS A COMMON material at the time because **flax**—the plant that produces linen threads—grew easily in the rich Nile silt. Also, cotton did not grow in Egypt, and Egyptian sheep were not the wool-bearing variety.

WHITE WAS THE COLOR OF PURITY, and white linen cloth was mostly used for clothing during the Old and Middle Kingdoms. At this time, the Egyptians sometimes used brown and blue dyes to color the linen, but were unable to use other, brighter colors, such as red and green, as they needed a special fixative to color the cloth. By the New Kingdom the method for fixing dyes had been discovered. After this clothes became much brighter and designs more elaborate.

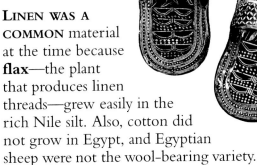

ANCIENT EGYPTIANS LIVED in the northeast corner of Africa. They were not tall, had dark eyes, straight, black hair, and coppery skin.

MAKEUP and perfumed oils were used by men and women and kept in beautiful caskets. Oils softened their skin and stopped it from burning and cracking in the sun and sandy winds.

EYELIDS were colored with green pigment, made from a crushed soft stone called malachite. Eyes were outlined with black **kohl**, made of lead ore mixed with water, to make them look larger, and to protect them from the sun's glare.

CHEEKS AND LIPS were stained red with **ochre**. **Henna**, made from the powdered leaves of a plant, was used to color hair, as it still is today.

MIRRORS WERE ESSENTIAL for all this making up and hairdressing. Egyptian mirrors were round and made from highly polished metal disks, usually bronze. Their shape and brightness made the ancient Egyptians think of the life-giving sun, and so mirrors were important as religious objects, too. By the New Kingdom the back of the mirror was often decorated with sacred motifs.

▷ *This bronze mirror dates from the New Kingdom. The handle is in the shape of a papyrus plant.*

🦅 〰〰 **MAKE A WIG**

You will need: 3 sheets of black craft paper (24 x 16 in.), scissors, glue, ruler, thin and thick doweling, and modeling clay, or wig stand

1 Make wig stand using thick doweling as shown. Cut paper strips for wig base to the width of a ruler. Fit, cut, and glue base band. Make crosspieces as shown. Glue.

2 Cut long, thin strips of paper. Wrap each strip around the thin doweling and run your hand along it. Remove the doweling and you will have a tightly curled ringlet.

CHILDREN'S heads were shaved, except for one long, braided lock which hung at the side. It was known as the "lock of youth."

◁ *On important occasions, the pharaoh wore a false beard of braided and knotted hair, hooked around the ears.*

FACIAL AND BODY HAIR was thought by many to be unclean. Women used tweezers to pluck their hair and shape their eyebrows. Noblemen at court sometimes wore short beards, although most men were clean shaven. Priests kept their heads and bodies completely hair-free.

You will need: black eyeliner, green eye shadow, red lipstick

1 Make sure that your face is clean and tie your hair back. Apply eye shadow from the eyelid to the brow.

2 Draw a heavy line around the eyes with the eyeliner, taking care to avoid any smudging.

3 Darken the eyebrows with eyeliner to form a straight line.

4 Apply lipstick carefully, following the outline of your mouth.

5 To take off the makeup, wipe with cotton wool dipped in an oily makeup remover.

3 Put the base on the wig stand and glue ringlets to base, starting at the base band. Use shorter ringlets for the front, and trim the fringe with scissors.

READY-DRESSED WIGS
were worn by many Egyptians who shaved their heads or kept their hair short. Elaborately curled and beaded wigs were worn on special occasions. The base was made from a net of woven hair with individual strands looped into the netting.

◁ _The higher a person's status, the more makeup and clothes worn. Servants were scantily dressed._

JEWELRY WAS WORN by rich and poor, men and women, and even some sacred animals. Elaborate costume jewelry was worn to adorn otherwise plain clothing and as a sign of social position.

GOLD AND SEMIPRECIOUS STONES were used to make expensive jewelry. Cheaper versions were made of glass and **faience**, a glazed composition made by heating powdered quartz, or sand, in molds. Jewelry often served a dual purpose: as decoration for the body and as **amulets**, or charms, to protect the wearer from harm. From earrings to anklets, the ancient Egyptians decorated almost every part of the body.

STONES such as carnelian, lapis lazuli, and turquoise were thought to have charmed powers.

△ *This collar was found on the mummy of the pharaoh Tutankhamen. Made of colored glass, it shows Nekhbet, the vulture goddess of Upper Egypt.*

∿ MAKE A PECTORAL

You will need: paper (8 x 7 in.), pencil, compass, thin cardboard strips ³/₄ in. wide, glue, tape, rolling pin, modeling clay, plaster of paris, paints

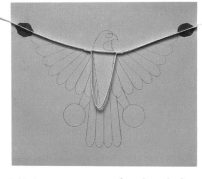

1 Using a compass for the circles, copy the shape above onto a piece of paper. Next, stick the strip that runs across the top of the wings and the body with modeling clay.

2 Starting with the body, cut, curve, and glue the cardboard strips so that they follow the lines of the drawing. Secure with tape if necessary.

3 Using a rolling pin, roll out the modeling clay. This will be the base for pouring the plaster, so make sure it is completely flat.

4 Place the cardboard outline on the modeling clay, pushing down gently so that no plaster escapes under the cardboard walls. Prepare the plaster.

5 Pour the plaster into the mold and let dry overnight. Remove the modeling clay, turn the pectoral over, and paint as shown right.

MAGIC MOTIFS included figures of the gods and, most significantly, the **scarab**—a representation of the dung beetle. To the ancient Egyptians, this was a powerful symbol of the sun god and life being reborn from dust. Children sometimes wore a fish pendant in their braids to protect them from drowning. Pregnant women wore figures of the hippopotamus goddess Taweret, meaning "the great one," to help them in childbirth.

GOLD-WORKING TECHNIQUES were quite varied. Most gold jewelry was made by hammering out thin sheets that were then cut to shape. These were decorated by punching on designs with a sharp chisel and making indentations to hold stones or jewels. The sheets were also cut into thin strips to make gold wire. Expensive, solid pieces of jewelry were made by pouring molten, or liquid, gold into molds.

▷ *This falcon pectoral with outstretched wings shows the god Re-Harakhty, the sun god in one of his many forms.*

talons clutch the "shen" symbol, meaning eternity

PECTORALS were worn on the chest for protection as well as decoration and often took the shape of falcons or scarabs. They were made using a technique now known as **cloisonné**, where semiprecious stones or colored glass are held in place by fine metal strips.

▷ *These gold bracelets show the god Horus as a child sitting on a lotus flower, between two cobras.*

From Pharaoh to Laborer

Egyptian **society** was well ordered and administered by law-enforcers, courts, and judges. All classes paid their taxes in goods or services, which were then used to pay government officials and the army. Scribes were the only members of society who could possibly rise through the ranks to become noblemen.

THE PHARAOH, meaning "great house," was absolute ruler. He could have many wives, but only one queen could be the Great Royal Wife. His symbols of office were the double crown of Upper and Lower Egypt, the **crook** and the **flail**, an implement used for threshing grain.

COURT OFFICIALS AND NOBLEMEN held high office in ancient Egypt and helped the pharaoh to rule the country. The pharaoh would often reward loyal nobles with gifts of land, so that they would have their own income from taxes.

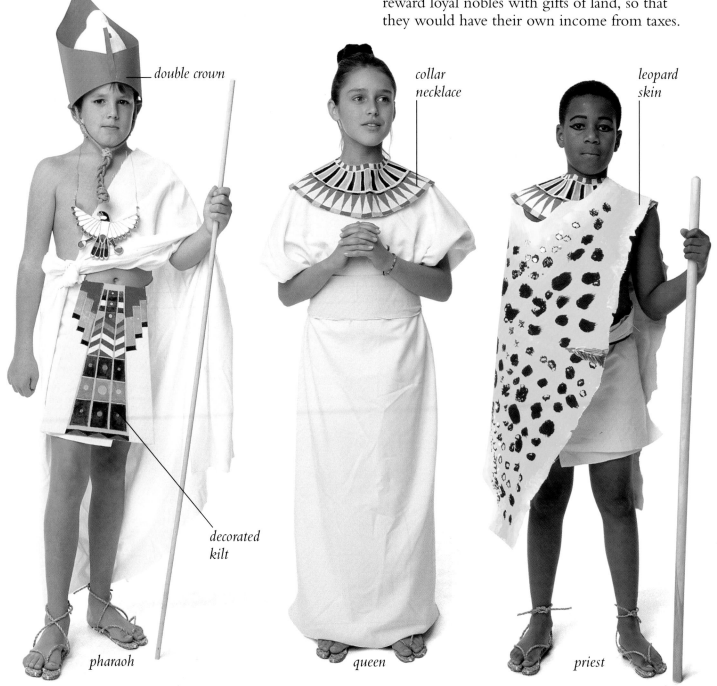

double crown

collar necklace

leopard skin

decorated kilt

pharaoh

queen

priest

PRIESTS AND PRIESTESSES looked after the temples and held religious ceremonies. The high priest ran his temple with the help of musicians, dancers, and assistant priests. People paid taxes directly to temples.

SCRIBES were the civil servants of ancient Egypt. They administered the law, collected taxes, and oversaw government projects. Parents were eager to send their children to scribal school (see page 41) so they would learn to read and write. They could then enter government or royal service where they might become rich and powerful.

ARTISTS AND CRAFTSMEN worked in organized workshops using simple techniques and tools and were employed by the pharoah, the government, or the temples. Blind people often worked as musicians during the Old Kingdom and dwarfs were traditionally employed as jewelers.

SOLDIERS AND UNSKILLED LABORERS came from the same social class. The laborers worked on farms during the growing season and paid their taxes in labor by joining the army or working on government projects during the flooding season when farming was impossible.

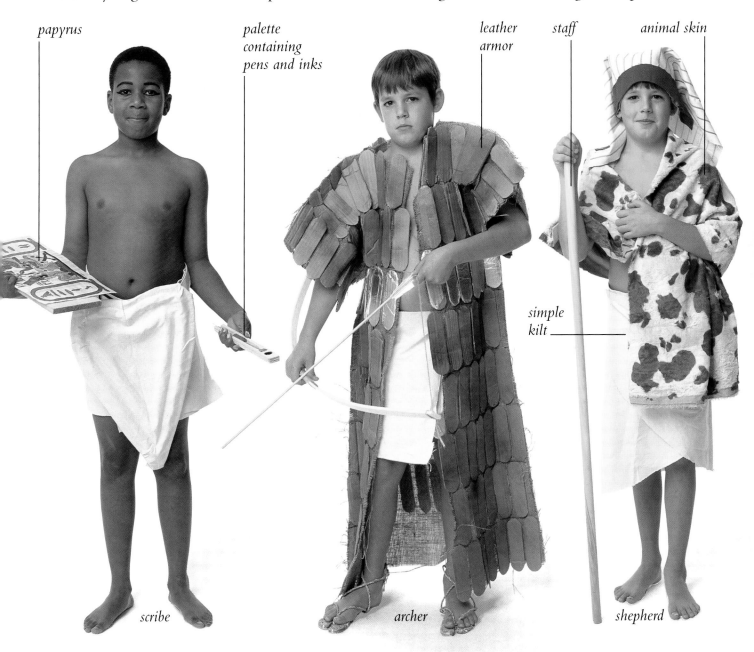

papyrus

palette containing pens and inks

leather armor

staff

animal skin

simple kilt

scribe

archer

shepherd

Homes and Villas ____

The majority of Egyptians lived in towns and villages strung out along the Nile Valley. To escape the effects of the annual flooding, towns were built on the edge of the desert and on patches of high ground within the cultivated valley. Until the New Kingdom, houses, palaces, government offices, and even temples were built from dried mud bricks, quite a fragile building material. As buildings crumbled, the occupants would knock them down and rebuild on top of the remains, so that gradually the high ground became even higher and therefore safer from the floods.

△ *This model "soul house" is based on a typical village house. It was placed in a burial tomb to provide a home for the deceased in the afterlife.*

〰 **GRANARIES, BAKERIES, AND BREWERIES** were important features of any town. Models of these buildings were made and buried with people when they died, as it was thought that they would need sustenance in the afterlife.

sun shield

silos for storing grain

silo

external stairs leading to roof

courtyard

outside granary

TOWN HOUSES were built with a shelter on the roof to catch cool north breezes. Families would sometimes live there during hot weather. Inside, houses were often cramped and quite dark as windows were small and high up to keep out the sunlight. Kitchens were usually situated on the top floor so that the heat and cooking smells could drift out through an opening onto the roof terrace.

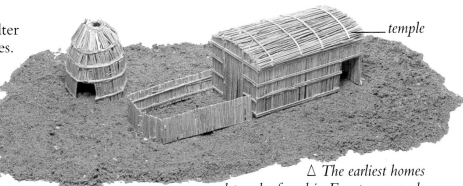

—temple

△ *The earliest homes and temples found in Egypt were made of reeds. The houses were shaped like beehives.*

SUPPORTING BEAMS and pillars were made of wood, covered in plaster and then painted. Columns were made of several tree trunks bound together with a rope made of **papyrus**, a tall reed. Houses were covered with a white limestone plaster to deflect the heat of the sun.

"TO START A HOUSE" was the Egyptian term for marriage, which was not marked with any kind of ceremony. Families would get together to arrange their children's marriages, and once a written agreement had been drawn up, the couple set up house together (see page 24).

ᎷᎷᎷ MAKE A VILLA

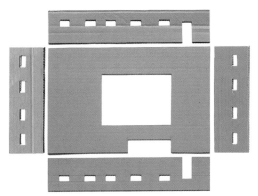

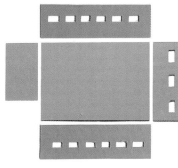

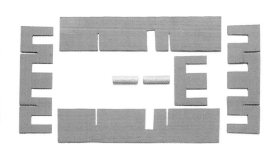

You will need: cardboard, craft knife, masking tape, doweling, plywood base, plaster of paris, sand, spatula, small pieces of wood

1 Ask an adult to help cut the shapes from cardboard as shown: lower floor walls and roof—12 x 8 x $2^1/_2$ in., and top floor—8 x 6 x $2^1/_2$ in.

2 Cut out interior walls for the top floor as shown above. Cut two pieces of doweling to the height of each ceiling. This is the column.

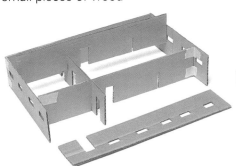

3 Assemble the lower floor and internal walls as shown. Fix the corners with masking tape. Glue column in position as shown on page 20.

4 Add the lower floor roof, then assemble and attach the walls of the upper story with masking tape. Glue column in place and add the roof.

5 Prepare the plaster of paris and apply a thin layer with a spatula. When dry, trim plaster from doors and windows with a craft knife.

A NOBLEMAN'S VILLA was home to family, servants, and livestock, as well as being a place of business. Like most Egyptian buildings, it would have been a low, white-plastered construction with a flat roof. Usually, this would have been approached through beautiful landscaped gardens with terraces, ponds, shady trees, and flowers. The vegetable gardens, stables, and granaries were situated around a courtyard at the back of the house with the servants' quarters and the kitchen.

▷ *The finished villa (see previous page) with part of the roof and walls cut away to reveal the interior. You could paint your villa, make simple palm trees, or use sand to decorate it.*

PRIVATE ROOMS were at the back of the house and were much more simple. This is where the bedrooms were situated and where children played without getting in anyone's way.

cool, enclosed central hall

thick, wooden columns

sun shelter

pool

dining area

shaded corridor

main gate

PUBLIC ROOMS were at the front and center of the house. This is where guests would be received and business was conducted. These were the grandest rooms, with high ceilings and decorated columns often inlaid with semiprecious stones. Walls were plastered and painted and hung with painted cloths. Floors were decorated with glazed tiles.

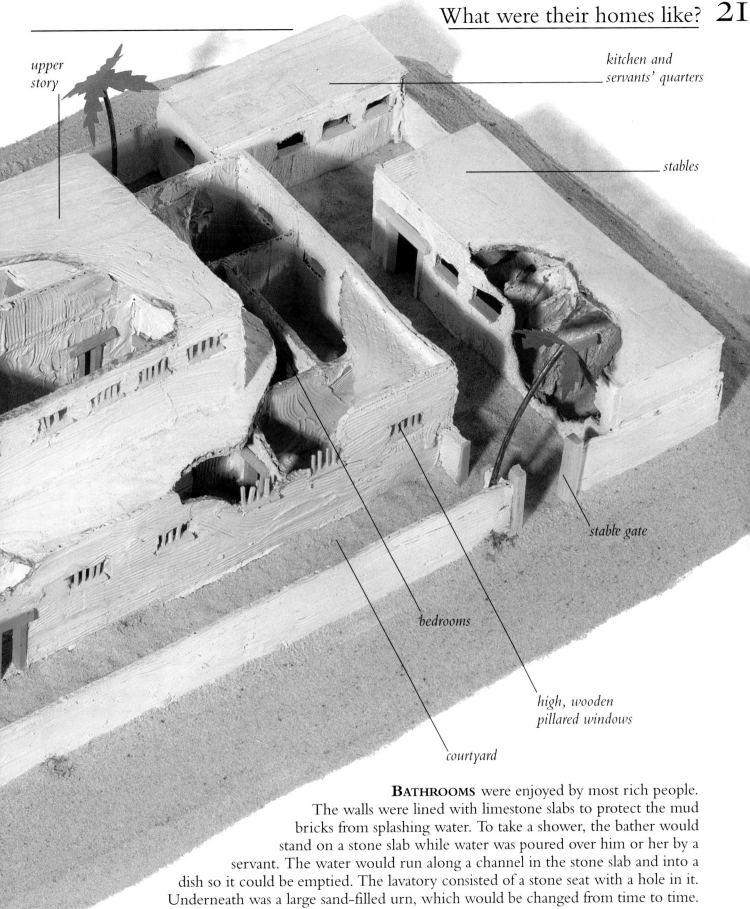

upper story

kitchen and servants' quarters

stables

bedrooms

stable gate

high, wooden pillared windows

courtyard

BATHROOMS were enjoyed by most rich people. The walls were lined with limestone slabs to protect the mud bricks from splashing water. To take a shower, the bather would stand on a stone slab while water was poured over him or her by a servant. The water would run along a channel in the stone slab and into a dish so it could be emptied. The lavatory consisted of a stone seat with a hole in it. Underneath was a large sand-filled urn, which would be changed from time to time.

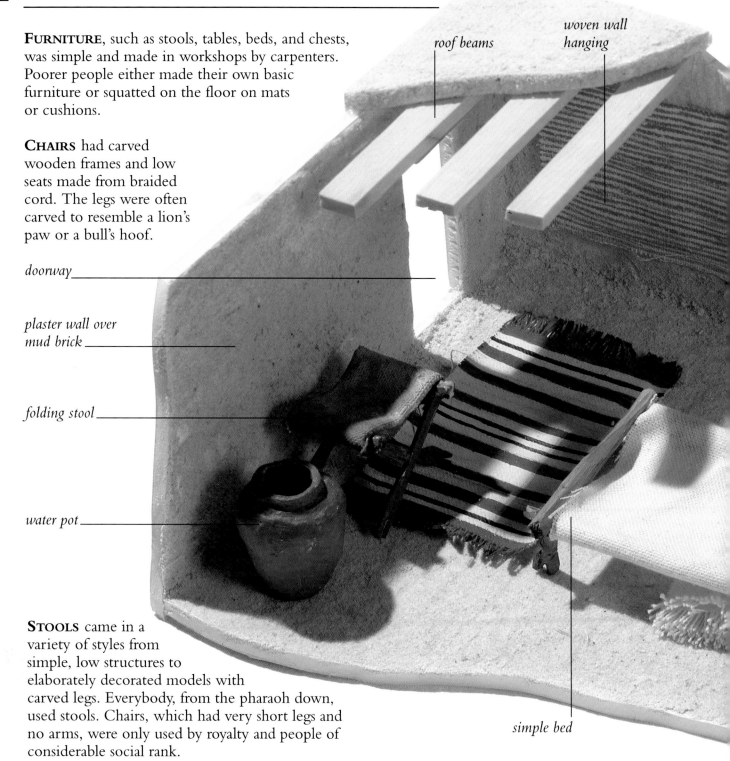

FURNITURE, such as stools, tables, beds, and chests, was simple and made in workshops by carpenters. Poorer people either made their own basic furniture or squatted on the floor on mats or cushions.

CHAIRS had carved wooden frames and low seats made from braided cord. The legs were often carved to resemble a lion's paw or a bull's hoof.

roof beams

woven wall hanging

doorway

plaster wall over mud brick

folding stool

water pot

simple bed

STOOLS came in a variety of styles from simple, low structures to elaborately decorated models with carved legs. Everybody, from the pharaoh down, used stools. Chairs, which had very short legs and no arms, were only used by royalty and people of considerable social rank.

LAMPS were stone or pottery bowls filled with palm-nut oil and a wick made of flax. They were lit in the evenings, only for the short time between sundown and bedtime, as people went to bed as soon as it got dark and got up at sunrise to make the most of the daylight.

MATS AND CURTAINS were made of woven reeds and decorated with colored fabric.

SHRINES to household gods were often a feature of Egyptian living rooms. Among them were Bes, the dwarf god of marriage and family prosperity, and Imhotep, the god of medicine.

CHESTS were used to store everything as there were no cupboards. Some were made of wood—sycamore, fig, or imported ebony—and some of woven reeds. They ranged from the plain and simple to finely carved pieces, inlaid with ivory and faience.

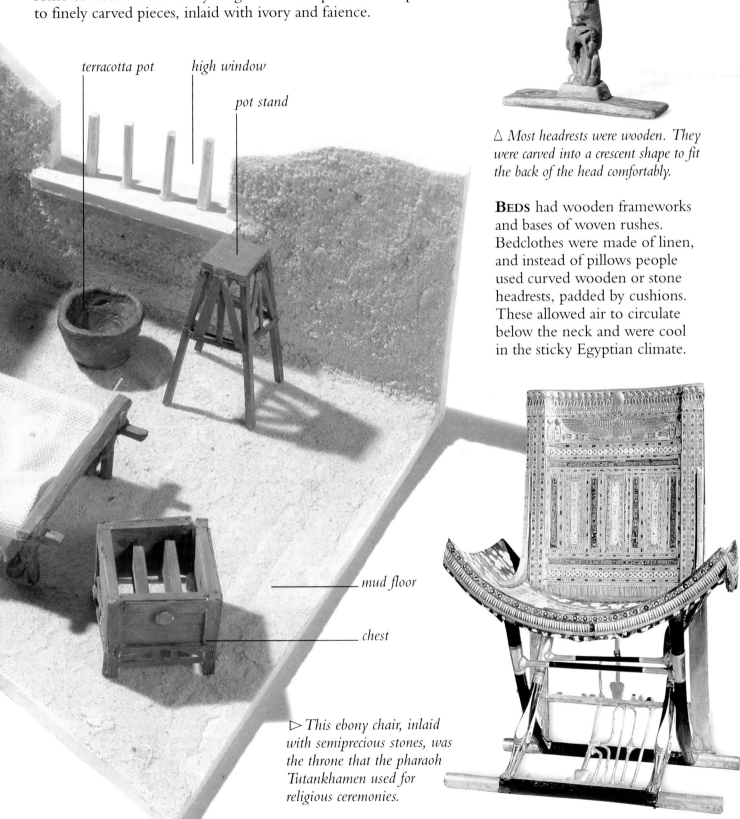

terracotta pot

high window

pot stand

△ *Most headrests were wooden. They were carved into a crescent shape to fit the back of the head comfortably.*

BEDS had wooden frameworks and bases of woven rushes. Bedclothes were made of linen, and instead of pillows people used curved wooden or stone headrests, padded by cushions. These allowed air to circulate below the neck and were cool in the sticky Egyptian climate.

mud floor

chest

▷ *This ebony chair, inlaid with semiprecious stones, was the throne that the pharaoh Tutankhamen used for religious ceremonies.*

Everyday Life

Ancient Egyptians had a strong sense of family and generally married someone in their own social group or extended family. Historians once thought that brothers and sisters sometimes married, but, apart from the royal family, it seems that this was not true. The words "brother" and "sister" in ancient Egyptian were simply terms of affection. Marriage was fairly straightforward and divorce was legal, but costly.

△ *This Old Kingdom tomb model of a woman and her husband, Hetepheres and Kaitep, dates from 2500 B.C.*

INTERMARRIAGES often took place within the extended family, such as between cousins. Children played an important role in society and were thought to be a great blessing. Parents prayed to the gods for many children who were expected to look after their parents during old age.

CHILDHOOD was short as children were sent to learn a trade, or the privileged few to be educated at scribal school when they were just eight or nine years old. Girls married when they were as young as 12 years old and boys at 14. The average life expectancy was 40 years, although mummies of officials and rulers show that some lived much longer.

DAILY LIFE centered around the marketplace, with stalls filling squares and lining streets. This is where the wealthy would send their servants to shop. The ancient Egyptians did not use money, relying instead on a **barter** and exchange system of trade. They used everything for this—from storage jars and furniture to grain, flax, or copper ore. Prices rarely went up, which meant that the value of things tended to remain the same. As a result, people knew what to expect in exchange for their goods.

cattle

market stall

white-washed
house

figs drying

▽ section of a typical town

flat roofs

narrow
streets

air vents

high, outer
wall

high, barred
windows

roof beams

wine stored
in cellars

TOWNS GREW UP quite
haphazardly around a central core
of public buildings. Houses owned
by members of the same family were
sometimes grouped around a courtyard
closed off from the street by a gate. Narrow
streets, up and downhill, linked the town together.
The streets were hot, dusty, and noisy, so people spent a
lot of time up on their roof terraces where it was cooler.

Work on the Land

Ancient Egypt was a wealthy country because most years the rich and fertile soil yielded magnificent crops. This was due to the annual flooding of the Nile River between July and October. During this time, little farmwork was done and poorer families paid their taxes in labor by working on government projects.

△ The **shaduf** was invented to lift water. A water container at one end of a swinging pole was raised by a counterweight at the other end.

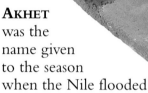

AKHET was the name given to the season when the Nile flooded the river plain, soaking the dry soil and leaving behind a fertile layer of black silt. If too little water covered the land, crops would suffer, while too much severely damaged houses.

WORK STARTED when the flood-waters began to recede. **Irrigation** channels had to be repaired and boundaries re-established. Farmers marked out their fields to avoid ownership arguments and to make it easier to calculate what they owed in taxes each year.

Nile

The annual flooding of the Nile irrigated and fertilized the soil of nearby fields.

Irrigation channels allowed the floodwaters to reach those fields farther away from the river.

PERET was the growing season and ran from November to February. Water had to be kept flowing in the irrigation channels to water the crops. Small boys chased off birds, but plagues of insects and flash floods were a constant threat to the crops.

SHEMU was the period between March and June, during which crops were harvested. Children worked, too, picking up the ears of wheat or barley missed by the harvesters. The work was overseen by tax assessors or scribes who calculated how much the farmers owed in taxes and rent.

THE LAND WAS PLOWED, once it had been cleared, by a simple wooden plow pulled by cows. The most important seeds sown were wheat and barley for making bread and beer, flax for making linen cloth and linseed oil, and emmer, an ancient variety of wheat.

HARVESTED CROPS were taken away to be stored in granaries once all dues had been paid to the government. Those who did not pay were often beaten without mercy. Finally, offerings were made to Renenutet, goddess of the harvest, as thanks for a plentiful crop.

The parched soil of the plains was covered with a fine layer of silt.

Deeper channels had to be dug in order to irrigate higher ground.

Towns and villages were located on high, dry ground to avoid flooding.

Food and Drink

The Egyptians loved good food and drink. Almost all their food was homegrown, and the staple food was bread. Most people drank beer, brewed from barley, and the rich drank wine. Even poor people enjoyed a healthy diet of vegetables, fruit, and fish from the Nile, while the wealthy supplemented their diet with meat— mainly from calves and oxen—and poultry such as duck, pigeon, goose, and stork. Meat was expensive because there were few grazing pastures as land was needed for growing crops.

△ *This coffin painting of a man offering a feast to the gods gives us an idea of what the Egyptians used to eat.*

EGYPTIANS DINED at low tables and ate with their fingers. Ordinary people ate off earthenware dishes, but the rich were attended by servants who served them on dishes of silver, bronze, gold, or faience.

During banquets the servants would tie a cone of scented grease on the head of each guest. These would melt and run down the guests' hair and wigs, leaving them sweetly perfumed.

MAKE FIG CAKES

You will need: food processor, 1⅓ cup fresh figs, water, ⅓ cup walnuts, ⅓ cup almonds, honey, ground cardamom

1 With an adult's help, use a food processor to grind the almonds and walnuts separately. Set them aside.

2 Chop the figs roughly and put them in the food processor, adding just a little water.

BEER WAS MADE by first half-baking loaves of barley bread, then crumbling the loaves into a mixture of barley and water. The jars were sealed and left to ferment, and the resulting thick, lumpy beer was strained through a sieve before being served.

THE GRAPEVINE was one of the main garden crops, and was used mainly for wine. Grapes were trampled to extract the juice in troughs big enough to hold six men. It was poured into clay jars and sealed and labeled with the date and the name of the vineyard, much as it is today.

▷ *Once grain had been harvested, it was threshed (trampled by oxen) and winnowed, to separate the grains from the chaff, or casing. Then it was stored in silos until it was ground down for cooking.*

COOKING was done outside or on the rooftops, because it was too hot and dangerous to cook over an open fire indoors. Fires were started by rubbing a bow string vigorously against a stick.

MEAT from cows and sheep was broiled over the open fire or stewed. Some pigs were kept, although priests associated them with the evil god Set, and they refused to eat them. Fish and ducks caught from the Nile were sometimes salted and dried to preserve them. Bees were kept in clay pots to produce honey, which was used as a sweetener in baking.

storing grain in silos

threshing grain

3 Add the walnuts and cardamom and blend again, adding a little water if the mixture is too sticky.

4 Spoon the mixture out of the food processor onto a clean surface. Shape the mixture into balls.

5 Roll the balls in honey and sprinkle with ground almonds.

BREAD was the mainstay of most people's diet, but it was a bit of a mixed blessing. The texture of Egyptian bread was fairly tough as it was often full of sand and grit that became mixed up in the grinding of the grain. Studies on mummies show that it was so coarse that it wore down the teeth of those who ate it!

Fun and Games

Tomb paintings and the **artifacts**, or implements made by people, that were buried with the ancient Egyptians show that they enjoyed themselves in many ways. Music was very popular, and performers were in great demand at celebrations.

MUSICIANS were mostly male during the Old Kingdom, but mainly female by the New Kingdom. Blind men were sometimes employed as harpists. Being blind was not a disadvantage because music was memorized by sound rather than written down. Children of rich families were also taught to play instruments for their own pleasure.

〰️ **MAKE A HARP**

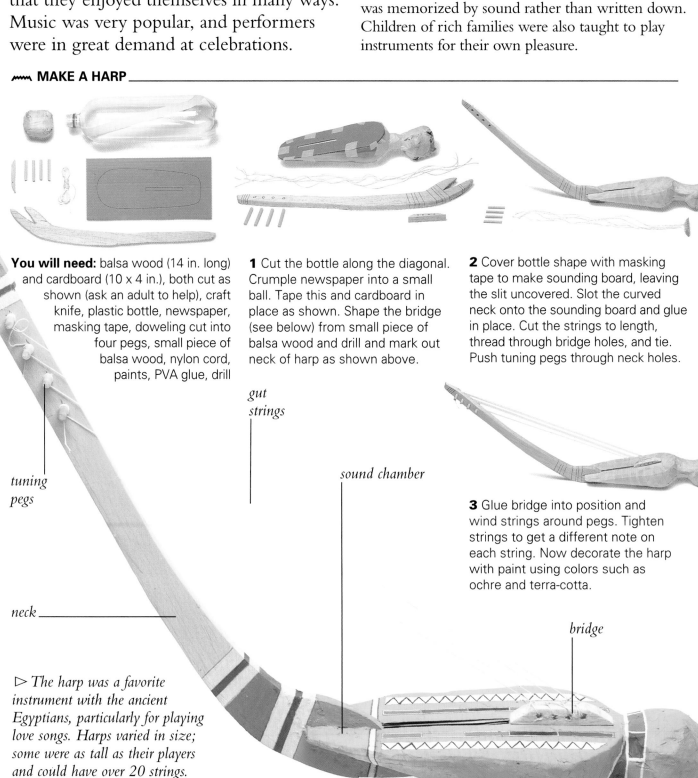

You will need: balsa wood (14 in. long) and cardboard (10 x 4 in.), both cut as shown (ask an adult to help), craft knife, plastic bottle, newspaper, masking tape, doweling cut into four pegs, small piece of balsa wood, nylon cord, paints, PVA glue, drill

1 Cut the bottle along the diagonal. Crumple newspaper into a small ball. Tape this and cardboard in place as shown. Shape the bridge (see below) from small piece of balsa wood and drill and mark out neck of harp as shown above.

2 Cover bottle shape with masking tape to make sounding board, leaving the slit uncovered. Slot the curved neck onto the sounding board and glue in place. Cut the strings to length, thread through bridge holes, and tie. Push tuning pegs through neck holes.

3 Glue bridge into position and wind strings around pegs. Tighten strings to get a different note on each string. Now decorate the harp with paint using colors such as ochre and terra-cotta.

tuning pegs

gut strings

sound chamber

neck

bridge

▷ *The harp was a favorite instrument with the ancient Egyptians, particularly for playing love songs. Harps varied in size; some were as tall as their players and could have over 20 strings.*

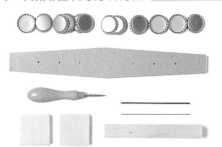

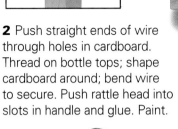

~~~ MAKE A SISTRUM

You will need: balsa wood (8 x 1 in.), PVA glue, saw, awl, pliers, thin wire, wire cutter, cardboard (16 x 3 in.) cut and holes made as shown, bottle tops, paint

1 Glue both squares of wood onto handle as shown. Use awl to pierce a hole in each bottle top. Cut the wire into three, using pliers to bend up one side. Make saw cuts into the top of the handle as shown above right.

2 Push straight ends of wire through holes in cardboard. Thread on bottle tops; shape cardboard around; bend wire to secure. Push rattle head into slots in handle and glue. Paint.

MUSICAL INSTRUMENTS fell into three groups: strings, wind, and percussion. They became more complex during the New Kingdom as new musical ideas arrived from the East. The harp, lyre, and lute were the main string instruments; early forms of the flute, oboe, and clarinet made up the wind section; rattles, castanets, and tambourines were popular percussion instruments.

△ *Dancing girls and musicians are in full swing at a banquet in this wall painting. The hieroglyphs show the song being performed.*

EGYPTIAN BANQUETS were rowdy and fun, and religious festivals were equally lively. Enormous amounts of food and wine were consumed, and for guests who overindulged, a servant was always on hand with scented water or a sick bowl!

PROFESSIONAL DANCERS, acrobats, magicians, and storytellers were attached to the royal court and to noblemen's homes. The dancers were mainly women who started their training when young. Other performers worked in troupes for hire.

△ *Noblewomen and priestesses carried a sacred rattle, or sistrum, at ceremonies.*

~~~ **HUNTING** was a favorite pastime of men. The pharaoh and his nobles hunted lions, wild bulls, and leopards. Accompanied by professional hunters, they took off into the desert in horse-drawn chariots in pursuit of prey. Alternatively, they would lie in wait around a water hole, ready to attack beasts with bows and arrows.

IN THE MARSHY RIVER DELTA, waterbirds were killed with throwing sticks, and hippopotami with lassoes and harpoons. Hippos were a menace to farmers as they flattened crops. Only the brave hunted crocodiles.

▷ *Hippo-hunting on the river*

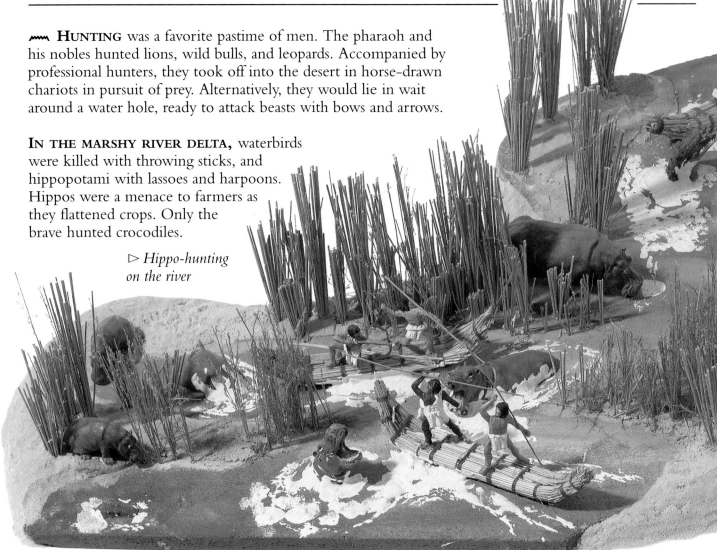

THE RIVER was also a place to relax. Egyptians would take their reed boats down to the water, enjoy a picnic, go fishing, or catch waterbirds.

CHILDREN played leapfrog and tug-of-war and practiced wrestling and gymnastics. **Senet** was a favorite board game played by everyone.

~~~ **MAKE A SENET GAME**

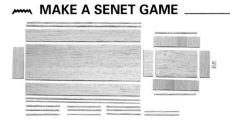

You will need: balsa wood, craft knife, PVA glue, paint, felt-tip pens, self-hardening clay, ruler, sandpaper

1 With an adult's help, cut wood as shown (12 x 4 in. base). Larger pieces (left) for board; smaller pieces (right) for drawer.

2 Make five pieces for each player (Senet is a game for two players) and a couple of spares, from the clay. When the clay is dry, paint five of the pieces black and five white.

3 Glue together the drawer and handle from balsa wood as shown. Then glue the drawer runners to the bottom edge of the side pieces. Mark the top board into 30 squares.

TO PLAY SENET

The object of the game is for one player to get his/her pieces around and off the board before his/her opponent. Players throw the four dice sticks to find out how far to move when it is their turn:

One flat side up = 1   Four flat sides up = 4
Two flat sides up = 2   Four round sides up = 6
Three flat sides up = 3

RULES

● Throwing a 1, 4, or 6 wins a player another throw.
● Pieces move up and down the board lengthwise: row one, left to right; row two, right to left; row three, left to right.
● Landing on a square occupied by an opponent means the opponent's piece must move back to the square his attacker has come from.
● Two pieces of the same color cannot occupy one square, but next to each other they cannot be attacked.
● Three pieces in a row cannot be passed by an opponent.
● The square marked 〰 means a player must go back to the square marked 🗝, and if that is occupied, go back to the start.
● The squares marked ⫿⫿⫿ , 🦅 , and 👥 are safe from attack.
● A player cannot move a piece off the board until all his pieces are off the first row.

START OF PLAY

1 Place a white piece on every other square of the first row and five black pieces on the squares in between.

2 The first player to throw a 1 moves the last black piece on the first row one square down. Then he throws again, free now to move any of the black pieces.

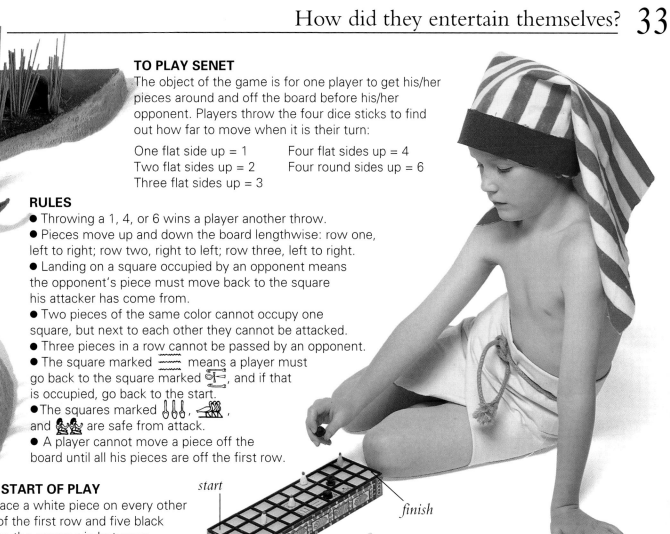

start

finish

3 When the white player makes his first move, he must use the last white piece in the first row.

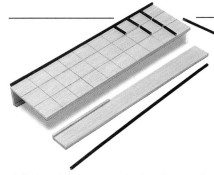

4 Paint the long vertical strips and shorter dividing sticks black. Cut the dividing sticks into short strips and glue firmly in between the vertical ones as shown above.

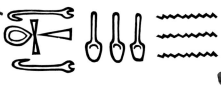

5 Copy the images above onto the top of the board. It is important that each sits on the correct square as shown right. Decorate the board's sides with felt-tip pens and paint.

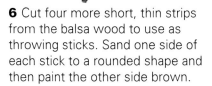

6 Cut four more short, thin strips from the balsa wood to use as throwing sticks. Sand one side of each stick to a rounded shape and then paint the other side brown.

Artwork

Many beautiful objects have survived from ancient Egypt, indicating that the Egyptians were skilled and creative. They made papyrus sheets to write on, and the rich adorned their houses with ornaments and fabrics. Many workers were employed solely as craftsmen to meet their needs.

WEAVING was one of the earliest Egyptian crafts. Scraps of woven linen have been discovered that date back 6,000 years. Linen fibers come from the flax plant. The stems were soaked in water until only the fibers were left. These were combed into fine strands and spun to make a continuous thread.

TO MAKE PAPYRUS SHEETS, papyrus reeds, which grew abundantly along the Nile, were harvested. First the green outer skin of the stem was peeled away. The inner core was then cut into strips and soaked in water. The wet strips were placed in a frame, side by side and just overlapping, and another layer of strips going the other way was laid on top. The paper sheet was pressed, dried, rolled, and polished.

MAKE A LOOM

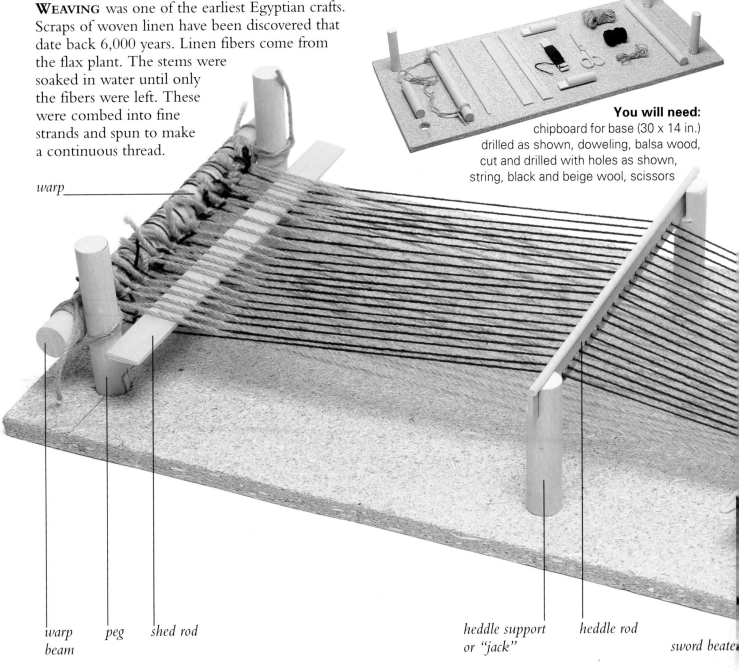

You will need:
chipboard for base (30 x 14 in.) drilled as shown, doweling, balsa wood, cut and drilled with holes as shown, string, black and beige wool, scissors

warp

warp beam   *peg*   *shed rod*

heddle support or "jack"   *heddle rod*

sword beater

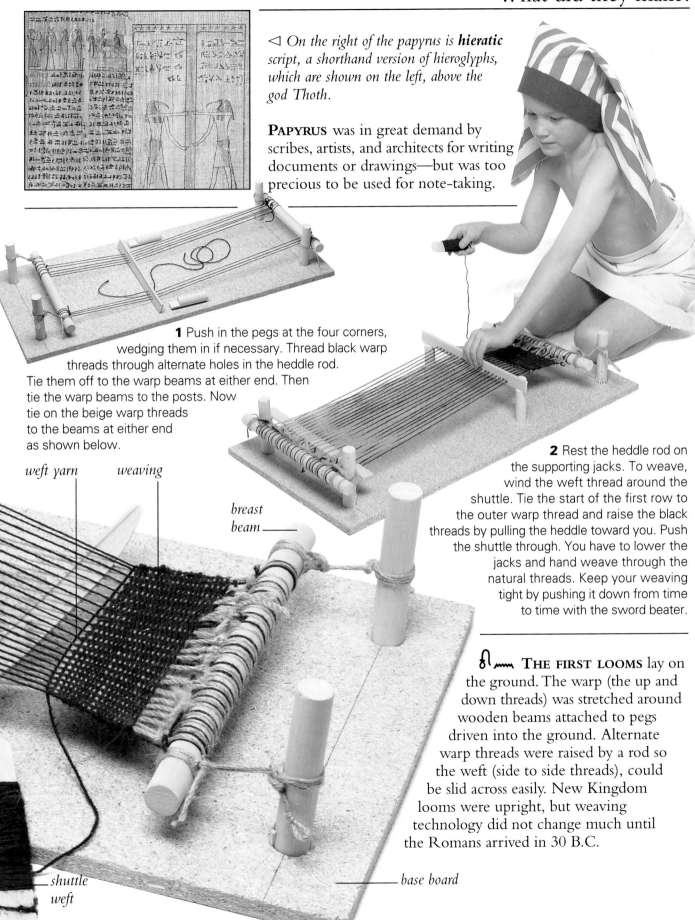

◁ *On the right of the papyrus is* **hieratic** *script, a shorthand version of hieroglyphs, which are shown on the left, above the god Thoth.*

PAPYRUS was in great demand by scribes, artists, and architects for writing documents or drawings—but was too precious to be used for note-taking.

1 Push in the pegs at the four corners, wedging them in if necessary. Thread black warp threads through alternate holes in the heddle rod. Tie them off to the warp beams at either end. Then tie the warp beams to the posts. Now tie on the beige warp threads to the beams at either end as shown below.

weft yarn   *weaving*

breast beam

2 Rest the heddle rod on the supporting jacks. To weave, wind the weft thread around the shuttle. Tie the start of the first row to the outer warp thread and raise the black threads by pulling the heddle toward you. Push the shuttle through. You have to lower the jacks and hand weave through the natural threads. Keep your weaving tight by pushing it down from time to time with the sword beater.

THE FIRST LOOMS lay on the ground. The warp (the up and down threads) was stretched around wooden beams attached to pegs driven into the ground. Alternate warp threads were raised by a rod so the weft (side to side threads), could be slid across easily. New Kingdom looms were upright, but weaving technology did not change much until the Romans arrived in 30 B.C.

shuttle
weft

base board

◁ *This Middle Kingdom jug shows a kneeling woman nursing a baby. Scholars believe that it could even be a representation of the goddess Isis feeding her son Horus. A mother's milk was thought to be a potent remedy for illness and was often stored in jars and pots.*

HOUSEHOLD POTS were made from river clay. The clay was first prepared by adding fine sand to make it easier to work. The potters then shaped the vessels using the coil method and smoothed them inside and out to a remarkably even thickness. The outsides of the pots were often rubbed with a flat stone before firing to give them a shiny red look. Others were painted with black designs or rippled by dragging a comb across the surface.

WOOD-BURNING KILNS were used to fire the pots. They were beehive-shaped and made from mud bricks. They needed constant attention to keep the temperature high and even.

MAKE A CLAY POT

You will need: self-hardening clay, sharp pencil, paints

1 Knead the clay until it is easy to work. Make a flat, round base for your pot. Keep the remaining clay in a ball so it does not dry out.

2 Take some clay from the ball and roll out two long coils of the same thickness. Score the rim of the base with a pencil so the clay will stick properly.

3 Use the coils to build up the sides of the pot as shown. Make a third coil before using the second, and so on, to ensure they are all the same length. Score every layer as you go.

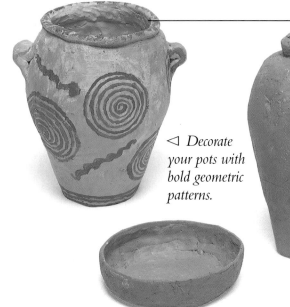

◁ *Decorate your pots with bold geometric patterns.*

A TAPERING BASE was given to many vessels. This meant they could be rested in a stand or fitted into a depression in the ground. Early on, they were decorated with geometric patterns on a red surface, or spiral and mottled designs to mimic vessels that had been carved from stone.

DECORATIVE VASES and stylized sculptures of human and animal figures were made in the New Kingdom period. Instead of the red and black decoration of earlier times, pots were also painted with a bold shade of blue, a pigment extracted from copper or cobalt.

◁ *A New Kingdom alabaster vase with a long neck inlaid with floral garlands made of glass paste.*

△ *This calcite "wishing cup" was one of the first finds by the excavators venturing into Tutankhamen's tomb.*

METAL VASES, BOWLS, and open containers were made of gold, bronze, and copper by hammering sheets of metal around an anvil, a heavy wood or stone block. Statues, tools, and weapons were cast by pouring the molten metal into a pottery or stone mold. All metals were considered rare and precious because, even if there was an adequate supply, mining was an expensive, difficult, and lengthy process.

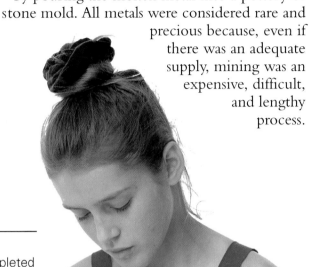

5 When you have completed your pot, smooth the outside and inside for a perfect finish. Add a rim and, if you like, a pair of handles. Then allow to dry according to the directions on the package.

4 When you get to the widest point, stop and smooth both the inside and outside of your pot. Score the top before you restart with the coils.

6 Paint your pot dark red to look like terra-cotta from the Nile Valley. When that is dry, paint on some black geometric designs.

STONE VESSELS were made from the large outcrops of attractive mottled stone found in the desert and hills bordering the valley of the Nile River. First, blocks of stone were cut out using a saw, and these were then shaped on the outside with chisels, **bow drills**, and **rasps**. Finally, the insides were drilled and chiseled out. Vases with narrow necks were made in two separate pieces and then cemented together.

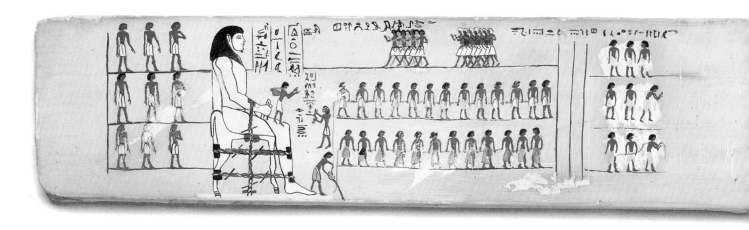

△ *This is a replica of a wall painting taken from the tomb of a powerful overlord from the Middle Kingdom. The painter may have first used a system of grids.*

THE BEST PRESERVED paintings were painted onto the plaster walls of the sealed tombs of the wealthy. Evidence shows that houses were painted with colored murals and patterns, also.

MAKE A TOMB PAINTING

You will need: plaster of paris, water, bowl, nail, polystyrene tray (6 x 4 in.), pencil, ruler, paper and tracing paper, paints, steel wool

1 Put the plaster into a bowl and add water gradually, stirring all the time, so that there are no dry patches of powder left. Mix the plaster with your fingers and get rid of any air bubbles.

2 When you have a smooth paste, pour the mixture into the polystyrene tray. Leave to set until it has formed into a plaque as shown above right.

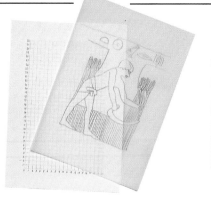

3 Copy or draw your own Egyptian scene on tracing paper. If you prefer, you can use the ancient Egyptian method of using a grid to help you get the figure(s) in proportion.

4 When the plaque is dry, put your tracing paper over it and draw over every line, pressing hard. Scratch away the lines on the plaque with a nail to leave a clear outline.

5 Paint the plaque using earthy, natural colors. Then, using the steel wool, gently rub away small bits of the picture so that it passes for being about 3,000 years old, as shown right.

◁ *A wall painting from the tomb of the pharaoh Horemheb that was discovered in the Valley of the Kings. The goddess Isis faces the pharaoh, and the god Harsiese is on the right.*

DRAWING, and the rules that went with it, evolved alongside writing. Artists drew and painted not what they saw, but what they knew was there. So if, for example, they were painting a chest that they knew contained a necklace in one of the drawers, they might show a side view of the chest with the necklace placed on top. And when they drew a scene, it did not simply record what they saw from their own viewpoint, but included everything and everyone that they knew to be present.

DEFINITE RULES applied to art because it had a definite purpose: to come to life in the next world. The people and objects in the afterlife had to be perfect, so tomb and temple paintings never portrayed death, disease, or old age.

PEOPLE AND OBJECTS were drawn flat, from whatever angle made them instantly recognizable. People were nearly always drawn with their faces, arms, and legs in profile (because they are easier to identify), but the eye and shoulders faced the front. Men were often shown as having dark skin, as they worked in the sun, whereas women were fair-skinned as they spent more time indoors.

PROPORTIONS were laid down so that people could be recognized by the gods in the afterlife and to provide guidelines for apprentice artists. Most apprentices used a squared grid as a guide. One Middle Kingdom scale measured the standing human figure as 18 squares from the ground to the hairline, so the shoulders started in square 16, the waist in square 12 and the knees between 6 and 7.

PAINT COLORS were made from powdered minerals and other natural materials. These are just some examples:

Black	charcoal
Red	ochre
White	powdered limestone
Blue	copper/cobalt
Green	malachite
Yellow	iron oxide

▷ *Malachite, an oxide of copper, was ground to make a soft green eyeshadow.*

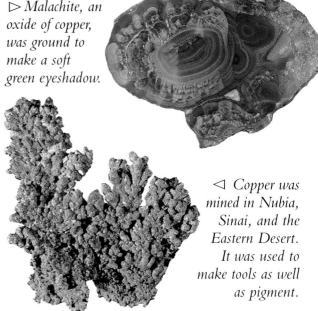

◁ *Copper was mined in Nubia, Sinai, and the Eastern Desert. It was used to make tools as well as pigment.*

Reading and Writing

One reason we know so much about the ancient Egyptians is because they had a written language and recorded everything. All legal and business agreements were documented, so the few who could read and write were in great demand. They were called **scribes**. Instead of an alphabet, they used 27 **hieroglyphs**, or signs, to represent sounds. There were an additional 700, which could be used in various combinations to give particular meanings or else to represent groups of two or three consonants.

ANCIENT EGYPTIAN belongs to a family of languages that spread across northern Africa and western Asia. Some languages in that family, such as Arabic, are still spoken today. But ancient Egyptian is a dead language, except where it survives in a form within the Coptic Church.

THE ROSETTA STONE was the key to deciphering hieroglyphs. This black stone is inscribed with text in three different languages: Greek, **demotic** script, and hieroglyphs. It was discovered in 1799, near Rosetta in the Nile Delta and later decoded by the French scholar Jean-François Champollion in 1822.

△ The use of hieroglyphs made writing complex and difficult to learn.

△ The top section of the Rosetta Stone is in hieroglyphs, the middle in demotic, and the bottom in Greek.

HIEROGLYPHS were carved into stone on monuments, painted on walls of burial tombs, and used for making up a **cartouche**, or personal seal, which could be used as a signature.

hieroglyphs   demotic   Greek

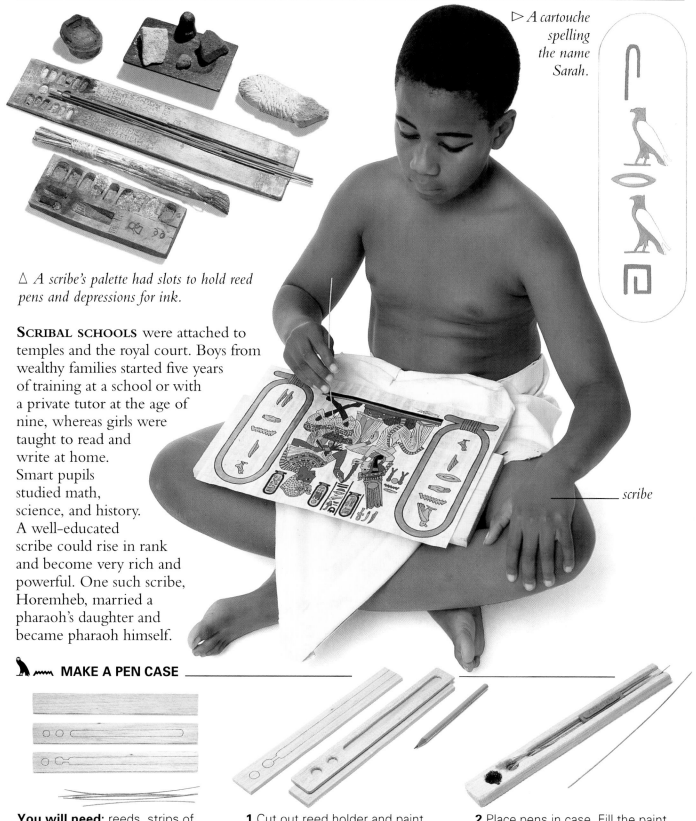

▷ A cartouche spelling the name Sarah.

△ A scribe's palette had slots to hold reed pens and depressions for ink.

SCRIBAL SCHOOLS were attached to temples and the royal court. Boys from wealthy families started five years of training at a school or with a private tutor at the age of nine, whereas girls were taught to read and write at home. Smart pupils studied math, science, and history. A well-educated scribe could rise in rank and become very rich and powerful. One such scribe, Horemheb, married a pharaoh's daughter and became pharaoh himself.

scribe

MAKE A PEN CASE

You will need: reeds, strips of balsa wood (10 x 2 in.), marked as shown, PVA glue, powder paints, craft knife

1 Cut out reed holder and paint wells as shown and sandwich together the layers of wood. Glue into place. Leave to dry.

2 Place pens in case. Fill the paint wells with powder paint to look like ground-up minerals. Now your scribe's palette is complete.

Egyptian Inventions

The Egyptians were clever, curious people who invented many things we recognize today. In addition to their complicated form of picture writing (see page 40), they had advanced ideas about medicine, measuring time, mathematics, and astronomy.

THE ANCIENT EGYPTIANS were the first people to organize the year into 365 days and the days into 24 hours. The Egyptian year was divided like this:

10 days = 1 week   3 weeks = 1 month
4 months = 1 season   3 seasons + 5 holy days = 1 year

THE WATER CLOCK, the most common Egyptian clock, was a vessel marked with lines on the inside. Time was measured against these levels as water dripped through a hole in the base. Sun poles, ideal in the sunny climate, were used by people of learning, such as priests, to tell the time.

MAKE A WATER CLOCK

You will need: pot made from self-hardening clay, painted and varnished inside to make it waterproof, awl, wax crayon, water jug filled with water, cup or glass

1 Make a small hole with an awl in side of pot near to base as shown left. Place glass or cup under pot to catch water dripping out of the hole. Pour water into pot, filling it up.

EGYPTIAN DOCTORS were surprisingly advanced for their time. Papyrus manuals reveal that they had a detailed knowledge of bodily systems such as digestion, circulation, and the nervous system. This was gained largely through centuries of **embalming** the dead. They also studied the symptoms of sick people in order to understand illness and disease and used plants and herbs, such as garlic and juniper berries, as cures.

MAGICIANS were valued for their healing powers, too. Spells were chanted as cures and to ward off injury, sickness, and danger.

▷ *The mummified head of Nebera, chief of the royal stables of Thutmose III. Embalming taught doctors a lot about* **anatomy**.

MAKE A SUN POLE

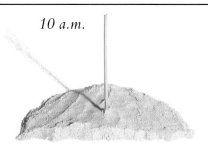

7 a.m.

10 a.m.

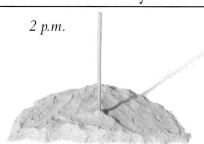

2 p.m.

You will need: wooden post, watch

1 Find a spot outside that is sunny all day.

2 Push the post into the ground and mark where the shadow falls at 7 a.m. Check the shadow's position every hour, marking it each time.

3 After a full day of sun, with a mark on the ground for every hour, your sun pole will be all set to tell you the time when the sun next appears.

2 Time the water as it drips out, using a crayon to mark the water level on inside of pot every five minutes. Once empty, refill pot and time again, checking marks for accuracy.

▷ *The Egyptian measuring system worked like this:*

distance from elbow to outstretched fingertip = 1 cubit

cubit = seven palms

palm = four finger widths

elbow to fingertip = 1 cubit

MEASUREMENTS were related to the human body. The main one was the cubit, equal to the distance from the elbow to the tip of the middle finger. It was further divided into palms and digits (the width of a finger).

MATHEMATICAL CALCULATIONS involving sophisticated **geometry** were used for building pyramids. The Egyptians had no signs for numbers between two and nine.

1= | 10 = ∩   100 = ℓ   1,000 = ⚱

so 13 was written like this: ∩ | | |
146 like this: ℓ ∩ ∩ | | |
　　　　　　　　∩ ∩ | | |

Boats and Chariots

The Nile was the highway of Egypt. Boats could drift downstream with the current to the north of the country and sail upstream with the help of the northerly wind to the south. The Egyptian hieroglyph for traveling north is a boat with no sail or mast, and for traveling south it is a ship in full sail.

𓊪 **EARLY BOATS** were made from papyrus reeds, bound with string made from reed fibers. By 3200 B.C. timber was being imported from Lebanon, and boatyards on the Nile were building wooden ships.

◁ *A gilded wooden sculpture showing the pharaoh Tutankhamen as a harpooner on a papyrus raft.*

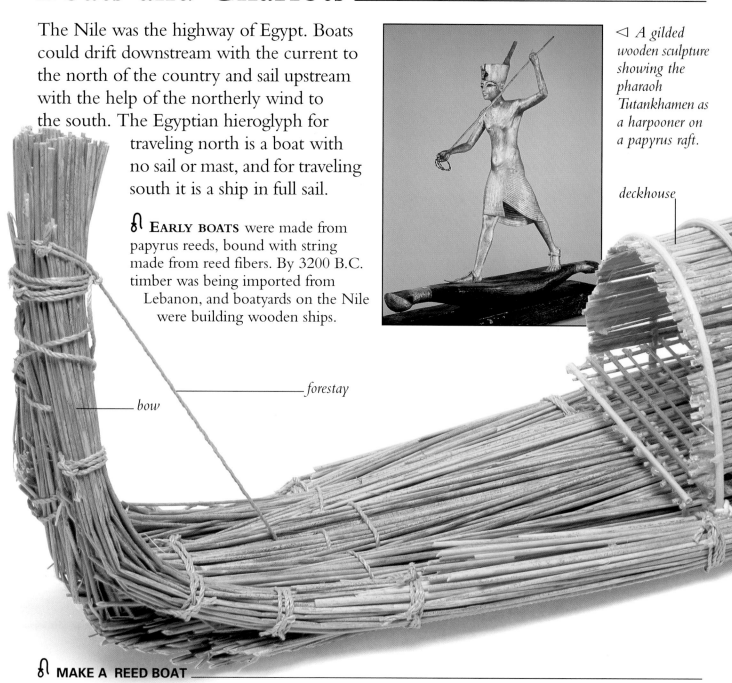

deckhouse

forestay

bow

𓊪 MAKE A REED BOAT

You will need: bundle of thin reeds or dried grasses 18 in. long, scissors, thin string, darning needle, balsa wood, cut as shown into handle and blade for steering oar, six lengths of basket cane for deckhouse (6 in. long), glue, scissors

1 Tie a small bundle of reeds with string at regular intervals. Prepare seven or eight bundles in the same way and sew them together. Trim the ends so the boat base looks like the example above left.

2 Make two longer bundles for the sides, as shown above left. Sew them on securely using the string and darning needle. Fill in the center with more bundles if necessary and sew them to the boat base as above.

FERRIES were used by most Egyptians wanting to cross the Nile, which had no bridges. A constant traffic of ferryboats rowed across from side to side, carrying people and goods.

GRAND BOATS owned by nobles and government officials were used for business as well as pleasure.

stern

THE SUN BOAT was believed by the Egyptians to make a daily journey carrying the sun god, Ra, from one side of the world to the other. It traveled along a river in the sky. At night, Ra was believed to sail through the **underworld**.

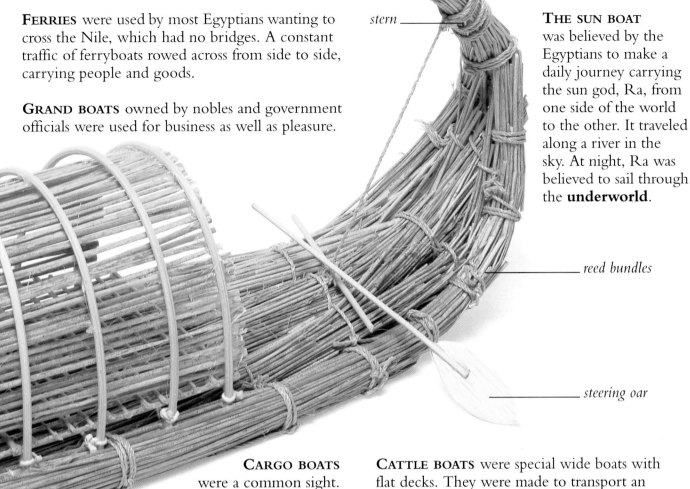

reed bundles

steering oar

CARGO BOATS were a common sight. All heavy cargo, such as slabs of stone or **obelisks**, was moved on huge river barges, towed by a fleet of small boats.

FUNERAL BARGES were used to carry bodies across the river to the embalmers' workshops. The crossing was conducted with great ceremony and dignity.

CATTLE BOATS were special wide boats with flat decks. They were made to transport an Egyptian farmer's most treasured possession—his cattle. These animals were the true measure of his wealth and worth protecting at all costs.

ROYAL BOATS ensured that the pharaoh traveled in great style and comfort. Huge, canopied boats protected royal families from the glare of the sun and the inquisitive stare of their subjects.

3 Shape the stern by tying the ends of the reeds into a tight bundle, curling them up and over and securing with string as shown (damp reeds bend more easily). Shape the bow in the same way.

4 The base of the shelter is made from a latticework of reeds glued together, and the roof from cane bent into semicircles, held in place with string. Fill in the roof from the inside with short lengths of reed.

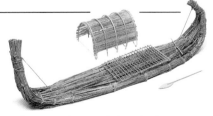

5 Glue the base of the shelter onto the boat and fix the roof on top. Glue together the oar handle and paddle. The stick at the stern is a support for the steering oar, so it can be held still. Now the boat is ready to float!

SEAGOING BOATS had to be bigger and stronger than river boats, although they followed the same basic design. They were built of wood, mainly cedar wood, which came from the hillsides of a seaport in Lebanon called Byblos. Seagoing boats were known as "Byblos-boats."

ORDINARY EGYPTIANS traveled very little. Some ventured as far as the next village and, if they could afford it, made a once-in-a-lifetime pilgrimage to Abydos, a religious center in the south. Generally, people were very suspicious of foreign places, and thought it far better to stay at home. Their greatest fear was to die in a foreign country where they would not have a proper burial, and so arrive unprepared for the afterlife.

△ A model sailing boat found in Tutankhamen's tomb, complete with oars and linen sails.

FOREIGN TRADE was the prize that tempted Egyptians to travel. To the south lay Nubia (now Sudan), rich in gold, copper, and semiprecious stones. Strange animals such as monkeys, giraffes, and panthers were brought back, too.

TO THE NORTH lay the Mediterranean Sea. However, the Egyptians stuck to the more familiar northeast coastline and traded with what are now Israel, Lebanon, and Syria. Syrians traveled to Egypt, too. Quite different in appearance, their colorful clothes and beards seemed strange to ancient Egyptians.

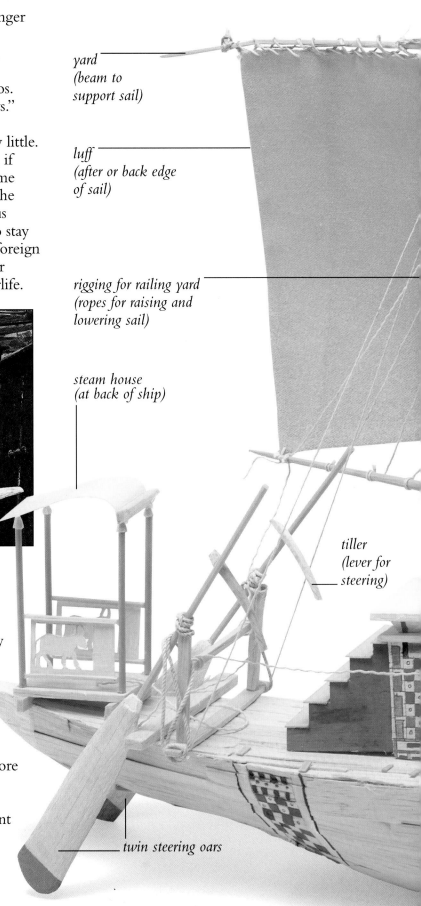

yard
(beam to
support sail)

luff
(after or back edge
of sail)

rigging for railing yard
(ropes for raising and
lowering sail)

steam house
(at back of ship)

tiller
(lever for
steering)

twin steering oars

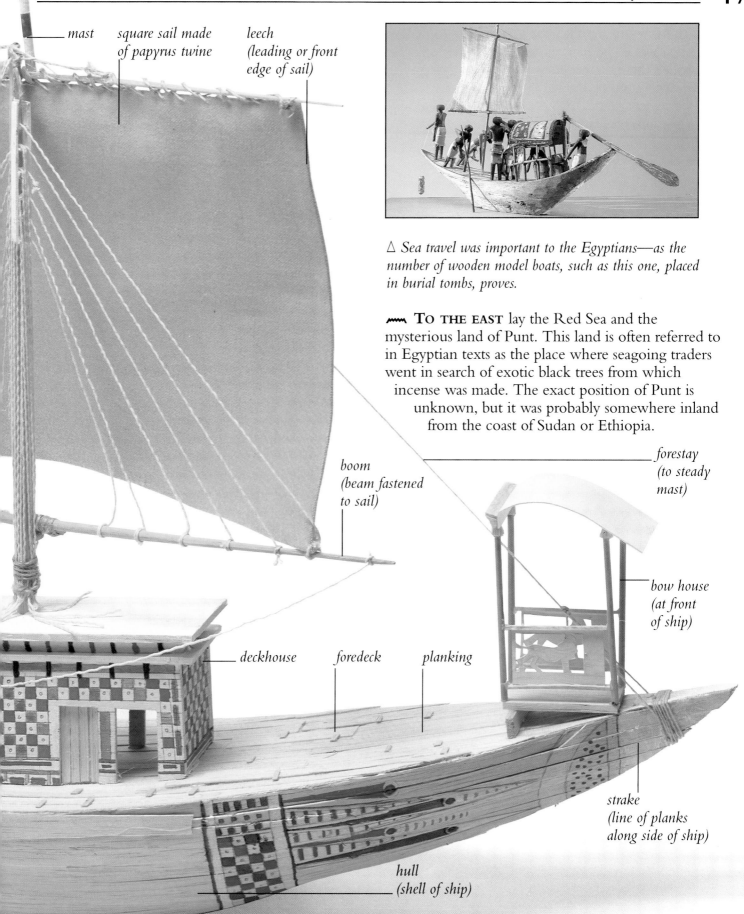

mast

square sail made
of papyrus twine

leech
(leading or front
edge of sail)

△ *Sea travel was important to the Egyptians—as the
number of wooden model boats, such as this one, placed
in burial tombs, proves.*

〰 **TO THE EAST** lay the Red Sea and the
mysterious land of Punt. This land is often referred to
in Egyptian texts as the place where seagoing traders
went in search of exotic black trees from which
incense was made. The exact position of Punt is
unknown, but it was probably somewhere inland
from the coast of Sudan or Ethiopia.

boom
(beam fastened
to sail)

forestay
(to steady
mast)

bow house
(at front
of ship)

deckhouse

foredeck

planking

strake
(line of planks
along side of ship)

hull
(shell of ship)

THERE WERE NO PROPER ROADS in ancient Egypt. There was no point as the annual floods would have washed them away. Unless they were lucky enough to own a donkey, ordinary people had to walk everywhere. Very rich people were carried around by servants on platforms with thronelike seats.

THE EASTERN DESERT, which lay between the east bank of the Nile and the Red Sea, provided overland routes to present-day Syria and Lebanon. Trade with these countries was important since they had a wealth of metals and semiprecious stones. The Eastern Desert also yielded raw materials, such as copper and tin.

〜〜 **MAKE A CHARIOT**

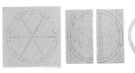 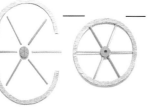 

To make the wheels you will need: paper, pencil, compass, balsa wood, thin doweling for spokes and pegs, thicker doweling for axle, wood circles for hubs, PVA glue, craft knife

1 Draw template for wheels as shown. Use the compass to mark two sections for each wheel onto wood (6 in. diameter). Ask an adult to help cut them out.

2 Assemble wheels, fitting spokes into holes drilled in hub and gluing them onto inside rim of wheel. Fix axle with peg as shown. Paint.

HEAVY OBJECTS, such as stones and statues, were tied onto sleds and pulled by men with ropes. Water or oil was poured under the front of the sled to make it slide along more easily.

horse yoke

TO THE WEST lay a desert area populated by **nomadic** tribes and known, during the years of the Old and Middle Kingdoms, as *Tjemehu.* Today it is Libya. Below Tjemehu was the endless stretch of the Western Desert, which protected Egypt from raiding neighbors. It also provided the ancient Egyptians with limestone which they quarried from the areas close to home.

yoke pole

LONG OVERLAND journeys were made to carry out these trading operations with neighbors to the east, and for mining and quarrying operations to the west. Donkeys were laden with goods and taken on long treks across the desert. Camels, ideal animals for desert travel, were not introduced until the beginning of the Roman period in 30 B.C. when raiding tribesmen descended upon the fertile Nile Valley on these strange, swift-footed beasts.

◁ *This relief in the rock, from the temple of Ramses II, shows the pharaoh riding into battle on a chariot while conquering Nubia, situated to the south.*

THE CHARIOT was introduced to Egypt by the Hyksos from southern Palestine. They invaded the delta area of Egypt at the end of the Middle Kingdom period. The rich were the only people able to afford chariots. They used them for hunting and traveling around on business.

CHARIOT WHEELS were a technological marvel, given the few tools available. They were made from curved segments of wood, bound together with a leather hoop. Initially, all chariots ran on four-spoked wheels, but during the New Kingdom, an extra two spokes were added.

To make the cage you will need: balsa wood, cut and sanded as above, uprights and axle fittings as above right, string, basket cane, PVA glue

3 Glue pieces of wood together as shown. Fix cane handrail onto top of uprights with string. Glue and tie cane front struts to form Y-shape.

To complete the chariot you will need: canvas (8 in. sq.) cut as shown, glue, weaving cane, thin string, darning needle, paint, felt-tip pens

4 Space cane strips across frame, gluing at each end. Weave vertical strips through and glue to form base. Glue canvas sides into position and bind the yoke-pole joint with string. Slot axle and wheels into position and bind with string. Paint.

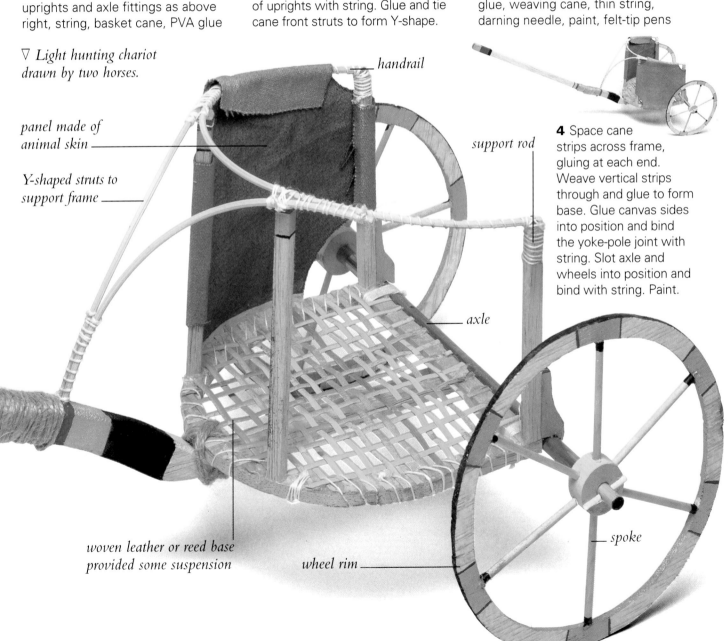

▽ *Light hunting chariot drawn by two horses.*

handrail

panel made of animal skin

support rod

Y-shaped struts to support frame

axle

woven leather or reed base provided some suspension

wheel rim

spoke

Guarding the Frontiers

△ *Daggers often boasted sheaths overlaid with gold.*

Ancient Egypt was the first rich and powerful civilization in history. Naturally it attracted the envy of neighbors who wanted some of Egypt's wealth for themselves. The pharaohs of Egypt would rather have conquered by influence than by war. But they were certainly prepared to push out the boundaries of Egypt, building fortresses for protection and dealing harshly with intruders if necessary.

MAKE A SHIELD

You will need: thick cardboard (30 x 18 in.), scissors, paint, canvas, pencil, string, PVA glue

1 Cut out cardboard in the shape of a shield as shown above. Then, cut out a piece of canvas, the same shape, only larger.

2 Glue canvas to cardboard. Draw a wide border around the edge. Paint the area inside the border white with brown patches to look like cowhide.

◁ *Arrowheads were commonly made of copper and designed to kill the victim instantly.*

battleaxe

THE ROYAL ARMY, during the Old and Middle Kingdoms, consisted of a small group of professional soldiers and the pharaoh's bodyguards. If a campaign was being mounted, laborers would be called up from the fields. At this time, the army was made up of foot soldiers armed with either bows and arrows or axes and spears and protected by large shields of wood or leather.

BY THE NEW KINGDOM, warfare had become much more organized. The army was larger and better run, with horses and chariots providing extra speed. Soldiers were well trained and were allowed to take slaves and goods from conquered armies after a successful campaign.

A golden fly was the pharaoh's award for bravery on the battlefield.

SEVERAL DIVISIONS existed within the royal army. Each division consisted of 4,000 foot soldiers and an elite corps of 1,000 charioteers. It was then subdivided into 20 companies of 250 men—200 foot soldiers (in four units of 50 men) and 50 charioteers.

CHARIOTEERS fought two to a chariot and were regarded as superior to other soldiers. They had their own barracks and were only temporarily assigned to a company.

AXES AND SPEARS had wooden handles and bronze blades. Soldiers wore protective tunics with metal scales or wrapped bands of leather around their chests.

CAMPS were set up when the army was on the move. A moat was dug around the outside and the soldiers' shields were used to make a wall.

OFFICERS' TENTS were comfortably furnished and they had cooks and scribes to organize supplies and keep a daily record of the battle.

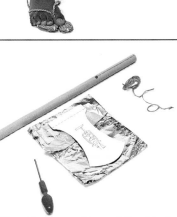

ᗡ MAKE A BATTLEAXE

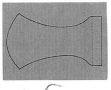

You will need: craft knife, glue, doweling, pencil, string, silver foil, saw, cardboard

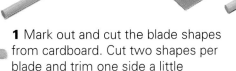

1 Mark out and cut the blade shapes from cardboard. Cut two shapes per blade and trim one side a little shorter than the other.

2 Ask an adult to help you saw down the doweling to the depth of the blade as shown. Score a design on the blade with a pencil.

3 Glue the two sides of the blade together with the longer side underneath. Cover the blade with foil, rubbing over the design. Slot blade into the doweling and secure with string as shown left.

Gods and the Afterlife

The ancient Egyptians believed strongly in many gods who ruled everything from the sun and moon, to love, wisdom, and war. Some were national gods, worshiped in grand temples all over the country, but most were local gods with temples in their own home town. Their strongest belief was that the Egyptians would enjoy a wonderful, trouble-free life after death, in other words a perfect version of life on earth. To be prepared, the dead were buried with all their possessions and food for the journey to the afterlife.

THE SUN GOD, RA, is involved in most Egyptian legends about the creation of the world. In one version, the world is nothing but a black ocean. Then a mound of dry land emerges out of the mud and a sacred blue lotus flower grows. It opens up and out steps Ra, who goes on to create all things.

▷ *An Old Kingdom group statue of the pharaoh Mycerinus between the goddess Hathor, regarded as the ideal of beauty, and Hu, the personification of a province of Upper Egypt.*

ANIMAL GODS were worshiped from the Old Kingdom onward. The Egyptians often associated the character of an animal with that of a god. By the New Kingdom, most gods continued to be depicted with the head or body of an animal.

◁ *A solid gold statuette of Amun-Ra, a New Kingdom god who was a powerful combination of the sun god Ra and Amun the creator.*

Montu, god of war

Amun, creator god

Khons, god of the moon

Thoth, god of knowledge

Horus, royal protector

Hathor, goddess of love

Anubis, god of the **necropolis**

Osiris, god of the underworld

HUNDREDS OF GODS and goddesses were worshiped by the Egyptians, and many of them were related. Shu, son of Ra, was god of the air. Shu's daughter, Nut, was the sky goddess. Her body stretched across the horizon, held up by her father. She married Geb, her brother and god of the earth. Their heirs were Isis and Osiris (god of the underworld), and together they ruled Egypt.

Set, brother of Osiris and Isis, and god of evil, was jealous. He murdered Osiris and cut up his body. Anubis, god of embalming and the dead, gathered the pieces and the goddess Isis restored him to life.

TEMPLES were the earthly homes of the gods and goddesses. Only priests and priestesses could enter, while ordinary people prayed at the gates.

〰 **MAKE ANUBIS**

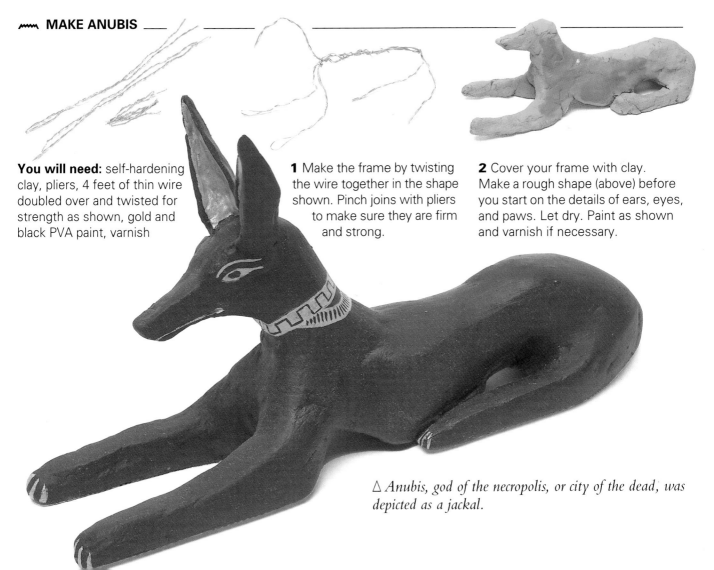

You will need: self-hardening clay, pliers, 4 feet of thin wire doubled over and twisted for strength as shown, gold and black PVA paint, varnish

1 Make the frame by twisting the wire together in the shape shown. Pinch joins with pliers to make sure they are firm and strong.

2 Cover your frame with clay. Make a rough shape (above) before you start on the details of ears, eyes, and paws. Let dry. Paint as shown and varnish if necessary.

△ *Anubis, god of the necropolis, or city of the dead, was depicted as a jackal.*

THE UNDERWORLD, called Duat, was believed to be a land full of dangers. The **Book of the Dead** was buried in tombs with the dead. This guidebook to the underworld, and a knowledge of all the right spells, guaranteed safe passage through the underworld to the Hall of Two Truths.

THE AFTERLIFE, an ideal version of Egypt, was where everyone wanted to go when they died. Upon death, an Egyptian arriving in the Hall of Two Truths would be led to a set of scales by Anubis, god of the dead and of embalming. Here, after being interrogated, his or her heart was weighed against the feather of truth. If honest, the person was granted safe passage to the afterlife by Osiris. The hearts of the dishonest were devoured by a goddess known as Devourer of the Dead. Paradise was no place for spirits without a heart.

GRAVES of ordinary people have been found, and it seems they were buried in reed or wooden chests along with their possessions and food, to ensure they reached the afterlife.

THE BODIES OF THE RICH were buried with a supply of worldly goods for eternity and models of servants to work in the fields of the gods to pay off heavenly taxes. Models of bakeries, workshops, scribes, and priests were also placed in tombs, so the dead would have all the help and guidance they needed. They also believed that the dead needed a body in the afterlife, which is why corpses were preserved.

△ *The magnificent death mask of the young pharaoh Tutankhamen represents him as Osiris, god of the underworld. It is made of inlaid sheet gold and measures 21 inches high and weighs over 27 pounds.*

MAKE A DEATH MASK

You will need: plywood base (16 x 12 in.); modeling clay modeled into a face, neck, and beard as shown above; petroleum jelly; papier-mâché made from strips of torn newspaper and wallpaper paste; masking tape

1 Cover the clay head with a layer of petroleum jelly, so the papier-mâché does not stick to it.

2 Cut out cardboard shapes for headdress as shown.

3 Start covering the clay head with the papier-mâché. Keep the layer of papier-mâché over the face as smooth as possible so the details of the features are not lost.

A BODY FOR BURIAL took 70 days to prepare. First the brain and internal organs (all except the heart) were removed and placed in **canopic jars**.

NATRON CRYSTALS (a type of salt) were packed around the body, which was left to dry for 40 days. Then followed a period in which the body cavity was stuffed with linen and sawdust, and false eyes were put in the sockets. The body was massaged with lotions and coated with resins. Finally, 15 days were spent wrapping the body with bandages and charms to ensure that the form was properly preserved.

A DEATH MASK completed the mummy. Royal masks were made of gold, while others were made of linen or papyrus and painted to look like gold.

THE LAST CEREMONY to be performed before burial was the opening of the mouth. The priest touched the mouth of the mummy with ritual instruments so the deceased would be able to eat, speak, and breathe in the afterlife.

◁ *The mummy of an adult woman which dates from around 1000 B.C.*

THE COFFIN, of either wood or stone, had inscriptions and prayers carved into it and usually a pair of eyes painted on the outside so the dead could see out. A little door was painted on the inside through which the spirit could leave.

4 Slot the cardboard headdress piece flat on the board, behind the ears. Place the top of the headdress over the forehead of the model and attach to back of headdress with masking tape.

5 Cover rest of mask with papier-mâché. Leave to dry. Ease the clay head out from the back. The beard and ears may be difficult to remove, so be careful. Now paint.

Pyramids and Burial

Pharaohs believed that they became gods in the afterlife, so their tombs had to be very grand. Pyramid tombs were built during the Old Kingdom. The shape represents the mound of earth that rose out of the dark ocean at the beginning of time, from which the creator god Ra emerged (see page 52). The biggest pyramid is The Great Pyramid of Giza. It is still one of the largest man-made structures in the world.

△ The Great Pyramid of Giza, the tomb of the pharaoh Cheops, was originally 480 feet high and took over 20 years to build.

△ Some experts believe that a long, shallow, mud and rubble ramp was used to haul huge building blocks up to the pyramid on sleds.

△ As the pyramid got higher, the ramp would get longer, to keep an even gradient.

covered causeway, nearly 1,000 yards long

valley temple

Nile

MARKING OUT the ground was the first step. It involved complex mathematics. To set out the corner blocks, the height of the pyramid and the angle of the sloping sides had to be calculated carefully. This ensured that the top would be dead center.

TO CUT STONES the Egyptians used copper and bronze tools (iron was very scarce). Another method was to make small holes in a block of stone, along the line to be cut. Wooden wedges were forced into the holes, and water was poured over the dry wood to make it swell up and crack the stone along the line.

TO SMOOTH THE SURFACE of the pyramid, great triangular facing blocks of the best quality polished limestone were cut and added to each course, from the top down. These facing stones gleamed white in the sun. The stone cutters were so skillful at cutting and fitting the blocks (they did not use cement) that even today a piece of paper cannot be slipped between two blocks.

subsidiary pyramid (for queen)

◁ *Pyramid complex of Sahure at Abusir*

enclosure wall

mortuary temple

ARCHAEOLOGISTS have various theories on how the Egyptians heaved two-and-a-half-ton stone blocks up a pyramid.

THE FIRST LAYER, or course, of stones was laid out all over the base. Side blocks were then laid out, meeting each of the corner stones. The next course was laid on the first, and so on up to 200 courses, until a single capping stone was placed on top. (In the case of the Great Pyramid of Giza, this was coated in gold.) Meanwhile, tomb chambers, anterooms, and access tunnels inside the pyramid were beaten out of the blocks with hammers made of a hard stone called dolerite.

THE ONE-RAMP THEORY suggests that a mud ramp was built and the stones dragged up it. But for the angle of the ramp to be shallow enough, it would have had to be three times as long as the pyramid, and no rubble has been found to indicate that such a structure ever existed.

THE ANGLED-RAMP THEORY states that the internal core of the pyramid was built in steps, and series of ramps were built from step to step. The steps were then filled out later with smaller stones, and the facing stones set into them.

THE LEVER THEORY proposes that teams of skilled workers levered the stones up the courses.

△ *The Great Sphinx at Giza is 4,500 years old. Over 240 feet long and 65 feet high, it guards the way to the pyramid of the pharaoh Khafre.*

INSIDE THE PYRAMID a series of passages snaked up and down and led to caverns and chambers, some lined with granite. Escape shafts meant the burial party could get out of the pyramid after sealing up the burial chamber and treasure stores.

△ *The coffins of royalty or noblemen were placed in a sarcophagus. By the New Kingdom, they would have the figure of a protective goddess carved into each corner.*

THE BURIAL CHAMBER was usually dug deep beneath the pyramid. Here, the coffin of the dead pharaoh was put into a stone box called a **sarcophagus**. Around the room were piled chests full of possessions, food and furniture, and models of anything an important person might need in the afterlife. On the walls, hieroglyphic spells gave the pharaoh safe passage in the afterlife.

ANTECHAMBERS were filled with treasures, so the pharaoh could enjoy a rich and comfortable afterlife. Boats were also buried with the pharaoh in case his spirit needed to travel.

AFTER THE BURIAL, the priests left the chamber, sweeping away their footprints as they backed toward the door. Then the door was sealed so that no one could enter.

THE MORTUARY TEMPLE was usually an unsealed chamber aboveground. Here, priests dedicated to caring for the dead pharaoh's spirit could leave food and offerings to the gods.

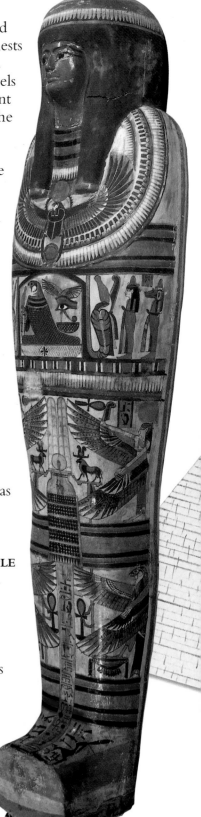

▷ *Coffins carried spells written in hieroglyphs, to protect the dead on their journey to the afterlife.*

TOMB ROBBERS have been raiding tombs for their gold, jewels, and precious oils ever since they were first built. The Great Pyramid at Giza, for instance, is thought to have been robbed of almost everything when royal power collapsed at the end of the Old Kingdom.

New Kingdom pharaohs felt that pyramids were too easy to break into, so they had their burial chambers built into solid rock. Corridors and chambers were dug deep beneath the ground and the pyramid entrance was well concealed.

◁ *Inside the Great Pyramid at Giza. The burial chamber was very deep to protect it from thieves.*

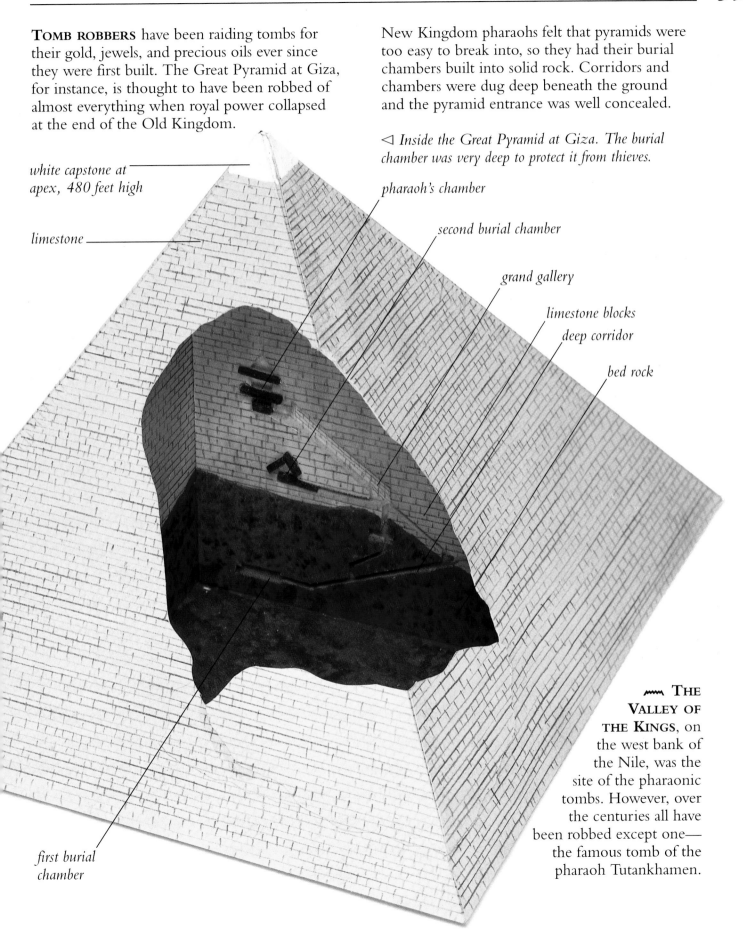

white capstone at apex, 480 feet high

limestone

pharaoh's chamber

second burial chamber

grand gallery

limestone blocks

deep corridor

bed rock

first burial chamber

〜〜 **THE VALLEY OF THE KINGS,** on the west bank of the Nile, was the site of the pharaonic tombs. However, over the centuries all have been robbed except one— the famous tomb of the pharaoh Tutankhamen.

An Amazing Discovery

△ *The entrance to Tutankhamen's tomb in the Valley of the Kings.*

THE DISCOVERY OF TUTANKHAMEN'S tomb in the Valley of the Kings was one of the most exciting archaeological finds of the century. The tomb had lain hidden from robbers since 1327 B.C.

annex—stored wine jars, oils, and food

We know a lot about the ancient Egyptians largely because they buried so many artifacts with them for use in the afterlife. As a result, their tombs reveal an enormous amount of information from which archaeologists have been able to piece together a detailed picture of their daily life. Also, Egypt's hot and dry climate is ideal for preserving these ancient sites and artifacts.

antechamber

descending corridor

sealed first doorway

FIRST EVIDENCE of the tomb was discovered in early November 1922, when an expedition, led by British archaeologists Lord Carnarvon and Howard Carter, uncovered a flight of stone steps cut into the rock face, leading downward.

stepped entrance to tomb

A SEALED ENTRANCE was found at the bottom of the steps; the door was plastered over and its seals were still intact. The corridor beyond the door was filled with stone rubble. Another door, the same as the entrance door, was also sealed.

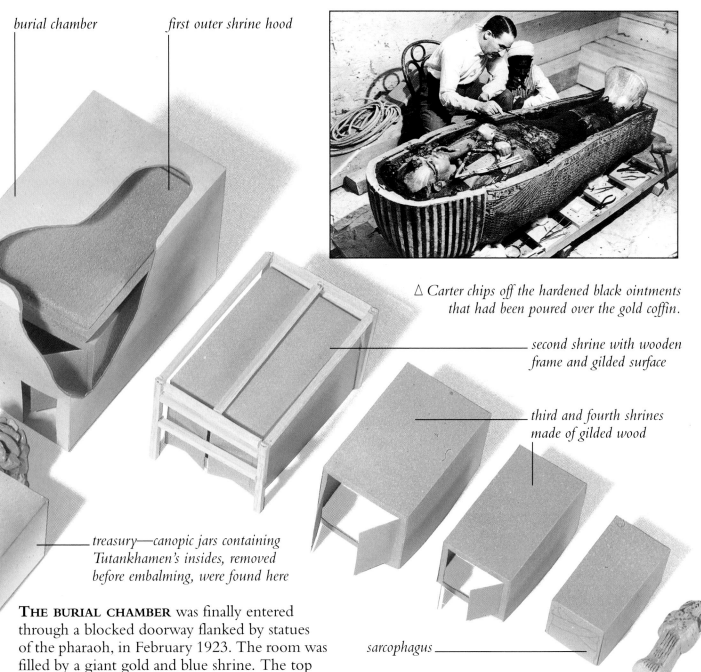

THE ANTECHAMBER was a stunning vision of glimmering gold. When, on November 26, 1922, Carter opened this doorway and held up his candle, he could hardly believe his eyes. The room was piled high with chests, caskets, statues, beds, chairs, chariots, and weapons. Clearing the chamber and cataloging all the objects took until February 1923.

THE PHARAOH'S BODY was brilliantly hidden. Bolted doors in the side of the shrine revealed another shrine and another. There were four in all, then a sarcophagus. Fitting inside this, like Russian dolls, were three coffins. The last, made entirely of gold, was opened in October 1925. It contained the 3,000-year-old mummy of Tutankhamen, wearing a mask of solid gold inlaid with jewels and garlanded with flowers.

burial chamber

first outer shrine hood

△ *Carter chips off the hardened black ointments that had been poured over the gold coffin.*

second shrine with wooden frame and gilded surface

third and fourth shrines made of gilded wood

treasury—canopic jars containing Tutankhamen's insides, removed before embalming, were found here

THE BURIAL CHAMBER was finally entered through a blocked doorway flanked by statues of the pharaoh, in February 1923. The room was filled by a giant gold and blue shrine. The top reached to the ceiling and there was only about half a yard between the shrine and the walls.

sarcophagus

inner coffins of solid gold containing mummy of Tutankhamen

Glossary

afterlife The ancient Egyptians believed that after death they would live on in a perfect world, if they traveled safely through the underworld.

amulet A piece of jewelry worn as a magical charm to protect the wearer against evil or illness.

anatomy The study of the way the parts of the body fit together.

anthropologist A person who studies the origins, development, and behavior of people.

archaeologist A person who studies the remains of buildings and artifacts from the past.

artifact An object made by people.

barter A system of trade where goods are exchanged instead of using money.

Book of the Dead A scroll made from papyrus reeds that was buried with the dead. It contained instructions and spells that would ensure a safe passage through the underworld.

bow drill A simple drill made from a flint or metal-tipped stick. A bow string is wrapped around the stick and pulled back and forth. This makes the stick turn, so that the sharp end drills.

canopic jars When a body was embalmed, the internal organs were removed and stored in these jars to protect them from spells.

cartouche A royal name written in hieroglyphs and surrounded by an oval border.

civilization A developed and organized group or nation of people.

cloisonné A type of decoration made by filling an outline of metal with colored enamel or glass.

Coptic Church The Christian Church of Egypt, established in the fourth century A.D.

crook A hooked staff which looks very similar to that used by a shepherd. It was one of the pharaoh's symbols of office (along with the flail and sceptre), and it represented kingship.

culture The activities, ideas, and beliefs of a group of people that form the basis of their shared way of life.

delta A place at the mouth of a river where the river splits into smaller channels, forming a triangular shape.

demotic A form of ancient Egyptian writing which replaced hieratic script around the seventh century B.C. It was quicker to use than hieratic and was used for legal documents.

embalming Treating a dead body using spices and ointments to preserve it as a mummy.

faience A glasslike substance made by heating powdered quartz or sand. The ancient Egyptians used faience to make colorful jewelry.

flail A tool used for threshing grain, which was one of the pharaoh's symbols of office. The flail represented the fertility of ancient Egypt.

flax A plant that is used to make linen cloth.

geometry The branch of mathematics that deals with lines, angles, curves, and spaces. It is an important part of architecture.

henna A reddish hair dye made from a plant that was thought to ward off danger.

hieratic A simple form of hieroglyphs used for everyday business, letters, and stories.

hieroglyphs A form of writing which uses picture symbols to represent objects, ideas, and sounds. In ancient Egyptian writing there were about 700 symbols, mainly used for religious inscriptions and monuments.

irrigation Supplying land with water so that crops can grow.

kiln An oven used for baking or "firing" pottery to make it hard and waterproof.

kohl A black powder made from lead ore (known as galena) which was used as makeup for the eyes.

loom A machine used for weaving.

mummy The dead body of a person or animal which has been preserved by embalming.

natron A type of salt used to dry out bodies before they were embalmed.

necropolis A cemetery or burial ground, often near a large city. Anubis was the god of the necropolis, as well as the god of embalming and death.

nomadic Leading a wandering life with no fixed home.

obelisk A tall stone pillar with four flat sides and a pyramid-shaped top used as a monument.

ochre A red, powdery form of iron oxide that the ancient Egyptians mixed with fat and used as makeup for lips and cheeks.

papyrus A tall reedlike plant which grew along the banks of the Nile. The ancient Egyptians used it to make a form of paper, as well as sandals, baskets, ropes and even boats.

pharaoh A king of ancient Egypt. The word "pharaoh" means "great house."

pyramid A large burial tomb with four sloping triangular sides which was built for a pharaoh.

rasp A tool with a rough surface used to scrape and file.

sarcophagus A stone box containing a coffin.

scarab A magic symbol in the shape of a dung beetle. It was one of the most powerful symbols because it represented the sun and rebirth.

scribe A person who wrote and read for a living. Scribes often traveled around on behalf of the government, recording information on the progress of building projects and the harvest.

senet An ancient Egyptian board game.

shaduf A device used for raising water from a channel in order to irrigate the land.

shrine A place where sacred images or statues are placed and worshiped.

silt Sand, clay, or other soil that is left behind by flowing water.

society People living together in an ordered community.

Stone Age The period when people used stone tools and weapons. It was during this time, in about 5000 B.C., that the first settlers arrived in the Nile Valley.

Underworld A dangerous land that the Egyptians believed they would have to pass through after death, before they reached the land where they would spend the afterlife.

Index

932
HAS

Haslam, Andrew. 2160800017

Ancient Egypt

DATE DUE	BORROWER'S NAME	ROOM NO.

$11.66

2160800017

932   Haslam, Andrew.
HAS

Ancient Egypt

HORACE FURNESS HIGH SCHOOL
SCHOOL DISTRICT OF PHILA

428781 01166   22444A   0005